We believe today's marke
that each one of us be ren
way that we serve our cus
companies and influence

Iconoculture is proud to be a sponsor of *The Big Moo*, helping spread the word of remarkable stories and secrets that inspire, stimulate creative ideas and serve as a catalyst for innovation.

Remember, remarkable is defined from the mind's eye of the consumer. As the leader in strategic consumer advisory services, we help our clients achieve remarkable growth by aligning their products, services, brands, and messaging with the consumers' wants, needs and desires – what they believe to be remarkable. We have a team of experts ready to bring you closer to your consumer than ever before. Let's do something remarkable together soon.

Dan Frawley, *CEO*
Iconoculture

Contact us at insight@iconoculture.com
or to learn more about us, visit www.iconoculture.com

Learn more at **www.remarkabalize.com**

The Big Moo

The
BIG MOO

Stop Trying to Be Perfect
and Start Being Remarkable

The Group of 33

Edited by **Seth Godin**

PORTFOLIO

PORTFOLIO

Published by the Penguin Group • Penguin Group (USA) Inc., 375 Hudson Street, New York, New York 10014, U.S.A. • Penguin Group (Canada), 90 Eglinton Avenue East, Suite 700, Toronto, Ontario, Canada M4P 2Y3 (a division of Pearson Penguin Canada Inc.) • Penguin Books Ltd, 80 Strand, London WC2R ORL, England • Penguin Ireland, 25 St. Stephen's Green, Dublin 2, Ireland (a division of Penguin Books Ltd) • Penguin Books Australia Ltd, 250 Camberwell Road, Camberwell, Victoria 3124, Australia (a division of Pearson Australia Group Pty Ltd) • Penguin Books India Pvt Ltd, 11 Community Centre, Panchsheel Park, New Delhi - 110 017, India • Penguin Group (NZ), Cnr Airborne and Rosedale Roads, Albany, Auckland 1310, New Zealand (a division of Pearson New Zealand Ltd) • Penguin Books (South Africa) (Pty) Ltd, 24 Sturdee Avenue, Rosebank, Johannesburgh 2196, South Africa

Penguin Books Ltd, Registered Offices: 80 Strand, London WC2R ORL, England

First Published in 2005 by Portfolio, a member of Penguin Group (USA) Inc.

10   9   8   7   6   5   4   3   2

The Big Moo is copyright 2005 by its respective authors: Tom Peters, Malcolm Gladwell, Guy Kawasaki, Randall Rothenberg (pages 99–103), Jackie Huba, Promise Phelon, April Armstrong, Polly LaBarre, William Godin, Julie Anixter, Dean DeBiase, Red Maxwell, Alan Webber, Heath Row, Mark Cuban, Dave Balter, Lisa Gansky, Kevin Carroll, Robyn Waters, Carol Cone, Lynn Gordon, Marcia Hart, Tim Manners, Dan Pink, Jay Gouliard, Marc Benioff, Donna Sturgess, Amit Gupta, Jacqueline Novogratz, Robin Williams, Tom Kelley, Chris Meyer and Seth Godin. Compilation copyright © Do You Zoom, Inc., 2005
All rights reserved

Cartoons copyright: gapingvoid.com

Publishers Note

This publication is designed to provide accurate and authoritative information in regard to the subject matter covered. It is sold with the understanding that the publisher is not engaged in rendering legal, accounting or other professional services. If you require legal advice or other expert assistance, you should seek the services of a competent professional.

LIBRARY OF CONGRESS CATALOGING IN PUBLICATION DATA

The big moo : stop trying to be perfect and start being remarkable / The group of 33 ; edited by Seth Godin.
     p.   cm.
ISBN: 1-59184-103-8
1. Marketing.   I. Godin, Seth.

HF5415.B448 2005
658.8—dc22   2005050909

Printed in the United States of America / Set in Electra LH with Univers / Designed by Daniel Lagin

CONTENTS

WHO YOU ARE IS WHAT YOU DO

You are not a cog.

You are not an assistant or an administrator.

You're not a gofer or a middle manager, either.

No, you're creative. A valuable asset to your family and your community. A person who can make a difference to an organization.

You are capable of having an impact, leaving a legacy, creating things that are outstanding.

You are not ordinary.

In fact, you're remarkable.

Now, hurry. Don't let yourself (and the rest of us) down.

"We have everything we need," she said, burning with Resentment.

© gapingvoid.com

PREFACE:
REMARKABALIZE IT

WHAT'S A BIG MOO?

Let's begin with the truth. Actually, we'll begin with *two* things that are true:

1. The only way to grow is to be remarkable.
2. The only barrier to being remarkable is your ability to persuade your peers to make it happen.

In the old days, showing up was 95 percent of success. If you offered a good product at a good price in a reliable way, you'd do fine. Being local was a good thing. Having a long track record helped. Decent quality and personal service mattered as well.

No longer. Good enough isn't good enough, because now *everything* is good enough. Our expectations of quality are unrealistic—and are being met every single day. We don't just want to be satisfied, we want to be blown away.

Not only that, but today, everything is a click away. Being local isn't good enough either.

Tiny churches are getting crushed by megachurches outfitted with energetic rock bands and complete day care centers. Copy shops, engineering firms, hardware stores, and ice-cream stands are being destroyed by bigger, faster, cheaper, or more vivid national operations.

If you're lucky, really lucky, you might be able to stay afloat, to break even, to somehow deal with the competitive onslaught as you try to do business as usual. You might be able to replace the business you're losing to your better-financed, bigger, and faster rivals. *But wouldn't it be better to leave that fear behind and grow instead?*

You will grow as soon as you decide to become remarkable — and do something about it.

> Remarkable isn't up to you. Remarkable is in the eye of the customer. If your customer decides something you do is worth remarking on, then, by definition, it's remarkable.

REMARKABLE OR INVISIBLE?

It's come to this. In our media-overwhelmed, hypercluttered, everything-is-good-enough world, your message can't get through. The story about your nonprofit, your law firm, your widgets, your corporate services — whatever it is — is being censored and obliterated.

A few years ago, I wrote a book called *Purple Cow*. It was all about why you need to be remarkable. The title came from a simple story about how boring cows are—and how remarkable a purple cow would be. Advertising cannot spread the word about your product. The only tool available to you is a fundamental one. The only tool left is to stop hyping the product and *to start making things worth talking about*.

Remarkable is not in the eyes of the marketer. It doesn't matter one bit how hard you worked on something or how cool you think it is. It's up to the consumer. If the consumer thinks it's worth remarking about, then you've got a purple cow.

Every once in a while, though, a product or service is so remarkable that it changes the game. Your innovation becomes something even bigger than a purple cow.

A few months after the book came out, I ran into a group that was brainstorming about ways to make their company remarkable. After a while, one participant blurted out, "That's not good enough. We need to create a big moo!"

A big moo is the extreme purple cow, the remarkable innovation that completely changes the game.

The idea stuck with me. Yes, a purple cow is what you need, but the big moo goes a step further. In order to grow at the pace the markets demand, you and your colleagues must find the big moo, the insight that is so astounding that people can't help but remark on it. In the same way that FedEx changed the world when they popularized overnight shipping, you can shake up your industry by breaking all the rules. By introducing the big moo.

You must remarkabalize your organization. Create a culture

where the big moo shows up on a regular basis, where "normal" is nothing but the short pause between remarkable innovations. In fact, where normal is gone and where the new normal is a constant stream of industry-busting insights and remarkable innovations that keep your organization growing.

Would you rather work at Just Marketing, Inc., or at Krispy Kreme?

Just Marketing is an advertising and marketing agency that focuses exclusively on motor sports. They represent companies that sponsor NASCAR, Indy and other races. Their clients include Subway Restaurants, Diageo, Henkel, Volkswagen of America, Merrill Lynch, Time, Inc., Travelodge, Jackson Hewitt Tax Service, Eli Lilly and Company, and Armor All/STP Products Company.

Two years ago, Just Marketing had eighteen employees. Today, they have fifty employees and they're almost done building a new office that will house one hundred people.

Krispy Kreme, of course, is the famous doughnut franchise that has recently seen its stock decline 80 percent, has fired its CEO, and is now facing store closings and layoffs.

My guess is that the answer is pretty obvious. For your career and for your peace of mind, the choice is clear. Even though the traditional choice is to work for the big company, the public company, the company that everyone has heard of and that seemingly offers security for the long haul, we're too smart for that now. Today, people realize that real security comes from growth.

Our economy is built around organizations that grow. Stocks

go up when companies grow. Lives are saved when philanthropic organizations grow. Careers are built and progress is made when growth happens. Things that grow don't grow forever—but that's okay, because the experiences we collect stick with us, and we get to take those experiences wherever we go.

My best job ever was at Spinnaker Software. I started in 1983, as the thirtieth employee. When I drove from California to Boston to start work, I passed a Spinnaker billboard in Chicago. "Yikes, this is a big company," I thought. It turned out that this was their one and only billboard in the country—they had built it for a trade show.

A year and a half later, the company had tripled in size and I was already working on my fourth cool project. If I had been required to wait for someone to retire in order to do something new and interesting, I'd probably still be waiting. Musical chairs takes a long time to win if you have a lot of chairs. Instead, the fast growth of the company gave me all sorts of opportunities to develop my skills and my career.

Wanting growth and *attaining* growth, though, are two different things. Most organizations are paralyzed, stuck in a rut, staring at the growth paradox. On one hand, they understand all the good things that will come with growth. On the other, they're afraid, petrified that growth means change, change means risk, and risk could mean death. Nobody wants to screw up and ruin a good thing, so the organization just sits there, motionless.

The growth paradox is endemic, afflicting nonprofits, big

companies, start-ups, and even individuals. It continues to frustrate millions of employees (and investors).

How can we get you to embrace the idea of the purple cow? How can we help you understand that your quest for the big moo—for the game-changing innovation—is the main reason (no, not the main reason, the *only* reason) you went to work today?

There isn't a logical, proven, step-by-step formula you can follow. Instead, there's a chaotic path through the woods, a path that includes side routes encompassing customer service, unconventional dedication, unparalleled leadership, and daring to dream. Is this a path worth staying on? Only if you want to grow. Only if you're tired of being a cog in a dehumanizing machine. Only if you are willing to embrace the quest for the big moo.

Seth Godin
Editor
Somewhere near New York, October 2005

INTRODUCTION: THE PURPLE LEAGUE OF AMERICA

Some kids dream of making it to the big leagues. They imagine that John Elway just threw them the football, or that Pele just kicked a ball at their head. Others, holed up in the attic, read comic books about collaborations between Aquaman, Wonder Woman and Green Lantern. You know, the Justice League of America.

My dream was to write a book with folks like Tom Peters and Malcolm Gladwell and Jacqueline Novogratz. Twisted, but true.

A few years ago, after I wrote *Purple Cow*, I started to hear from readers who wanted me to tell them "the secret." It wasn't clear to me what the secret was, but some thought there was a closely-guarded magic spell that would cause a purple cow to appear in their organization.

It's obvious (at least to me) that there is no secret, and, at the same time, that there are 85,000 secrets. Of course there isn't just *one* thing that'll work. Everyone needs to hear a different message. If I could just find the right incantation for the right person at the right time, I'd be a hero.

This is hard work. Finding the secret path for 85,000 different people is daunting. So I did the obvious thing—I asked the smartest people I know to help.

I got help from people you've heard of and from some who may be strangers to you. What they all have in common is this: They live and breathe what they write about. No posturing, no hypothetical nonsense.

Together, the group has sold millions and millions of books. But they've also built entire industries, raised millions of dollars for nonprofit organizations, changed the face of mass marketing and industrial design, and taught the world how to use computers.

Lisa Gansky cofounded the very first commercial Web site. Promise Phelon runs a thriving consulting firm that teaches companies how to get their customers talking. Marc Benioff is changing the way every sales force in the world is managed. And that's just three of the thirty-three contributors to this book.

My selfish dream would be to have dinner with this group . . . every night. There's no way I could pull this off. Even if I could, I wouldn't be allowed to invite each of *you* to dinner. So I figured that putting together a collection of short essays was the next best thing.

When Lynn Gordon tells you about thinking differently, she's doing it with confidence—her best-selling series of card decks are proof of that. When Robyn Waters or William Godin talk about product design, you know from their work that they've been there and done that.

Randall Rothenberg knows more about advertising (and what doesn't work) than anyone I've ever met. Marcia Hart has figured out how to use architecture as a competitive organizational tool. And Jay Gouliard did more than invent Go-GURT—he changed the way giant organizations get innovation done.

Virtually every person I asked to participate said yes without hesitation. Part of this is due to the fact that all of our proceeds go to charity. But even bigger than that, I think, is our desire to get more people to understand how very cool it is to live out your remarkable dreams.

You'll notice that the individual contributions aren't credited. Pretty unusual, perhaps even remarkable. We did it because it makes it easier to read the book as a whole, to avoid being interrupted by the noise your brain makes as it shifts gears from one voice to another. That and it lets you guess who wrote what.

This is a book about how and why to grow. It is not a book of facts or logical reasoning. Instead of lecturing you about how important and wonderful it is to do scary, brave, and remarkable things, *The Big Moo* paints a very different picture for you.

My colleagues and I are intent on slipping some subversive ideas into your subconscious . . . ideas that will help you dream bigger dreams (though they might cost you some sleep as well).

We believe that one way to get past the growth paradox is to avoid addressing it head-on. Instead of warning you about the dangers of stagnation, or promising you the benefits of growth, we've decided to tell some exemplary stories instead. Stories that are easy to read, memorable, and, most important, useful parables for putting growth to work in your own organization.

———

Every word in this book was written for free. All thirty-three of the book's authors are donating 100 percent of their royalties to charity. The proceeds from sales of this book are going to:

- The Juvenile Diabetes Research Foundation
- The Acumen Fund
- Room to Read

You can read about these charities and see updated records of our fund-raising by visiting www.thebigmoo.com. You can also read more about the work of some of the authors in the Group of 33 by visiting www.remarkabalize.com.

When you bought this book, you also bought the right to photocopy as many pages as you like, as many times as you like. Go ahead and make five hundred copies of your favorite story and send them out via interoffice mail. You can also find a few of the stories in digital form at our Web site. Feel free to e-mail those to as many people as you care to.

Most of all, we hope you'll *buy* copies of this book for everyone you know. That's why we volunteered our services—we want to publish a book that sells in the millions, that creates a movement around building the big moo. You can find bulk pricing by visiting the www.thebigmoo.com.

Thanks for reading. It's time to remarkabalize your organization. Spread the word!

The Big Moo

HARRY HOUDINI WAS
A LOUSY MAGICIAN

Historians of magic are in total agreement about this: Houdini did hackneyed mechanical tricks, showed little evidence of talent, and had almost none of the suave charisma that the great magicians of his era had.

And yet when I ask you to name a famous magician, odds are you'll say, "Houdini!"

So, how did he do it? How did a lousy magician become such a spectacular success?

Simple. *He wasn't a magician.*

Harry Houdini invented an entirely different sort of vaudeville attraction. He was not a magician at all, but an escape artist. Crowds didn't line up to watch him cut a lady in half. Instead, they were fascinated by his taunting of death, by the way he used himself as the most important prop in the act.

One of his breakthrough performances took place in England. Houdini was challenged (by a renowned locksmith—something you don't see very often) to free himself from a new kind of escape-proof set of handcuffs. At first he hesitated, but, motivated by the cry of the public, he accepted the challenge.

After half an hour in a tiny, isolated chamber onstage, Houdini came back before the audience and asked that the cuffs be removed so that he could take off his heavy wool coat (he was sweating from the heat) and then replaced. The crowd angrily refused—Houdini would not be permitted to trick them. Unflappable as always, Houdini used his teeth to extract a razor from his coat, which he then dramatically shredded to pieces in front of the crowd. With a grimace, he returned to his chamber. An hour later, he emerged triumphant, holding the opened handcuffs over his head.

When Houdini made the decision to focus on escapes instead of magic tricks, it was considered professional suicide. There wasn't a market for escape acts. There wasn't a demand for it. *It had never been done before.* No one knew what it was worth and no one could tell him how long or how demanding his act should be.

Who could have imagined that Houdini would succeed by spending more than an hour and a half doing just one trick, in a closed room, out of sight of the audience? Where is it written in the magician's manual that the best way to become famous is to fake not only the outcome but the event itself (Houdini made those handcuffs himself and paid the locksmith to challenge him in the first place—it only took him a minute to open them when the time came.)?

Sometimes, making an original choice when there seems to be no choice at all is daunting. But this is often how the brave succeed while the masses are consigned to failure.

HOW TO BE A FAILURE

1. Keep secrets.
2. Be certain you're right and ignore those who disagree with you.
3. Set aggressive deadlines for others to get buy in—then change them when they aren't met.
4. Resist testing your theories.
5. Focus more on what other people think and less on whether your idea is as good as it could be.
6. Assume that a critical mass must embrace your idea for it to work.
7. Choose an idea where number 6 is a requirement.
8. Realize that people who don't instantly get your idea are bull-headed, shortsighted, or even stupid.
9. Don't bother to dramatically increase the quality of your presentation style.
10. Insist that you've got to go straight to the president of the organization to get something done.
11. Always go for the big win.

CHOPPING ONIONS

Call it the curse of the TV Food Network. Since the network debuted about a decade ago, enrollment in degree-granting cooking schools has almost tripled.

What's happening to all the graduates? Often carrying more than $50,000 in debt, they take jobs in kitchens, cleaning potatoes and chopping carrots. As you can imagine, this is hard work—and low paying! About half of all culinary-school grads quit the industry within three years. They know that they're not stars on the Food Network and realize that they have little chance of getting off the chopping line.

The reason for this overwhelming attrition is that these wannabe TV stars are playing by the wrong rules. The new secret of success is that winning the game has absolutely nothing to do with hard work and paying your dues. In the old days, stable industries offered young workers a pyramid structure. If you did the work and stuck it out, you'd move up. Thirty or forty years after starting in the mail room, you'd be a senior vice president, an executive director, a bishop, or a chef with his own restaurant.

In our fast-moving, media-crazed culture, the opposite is now true. *Those who fit in now won't stand out later.* Those who follow the rules are never noticed—because the system has broken their spirit. There's plenty of work for the undifferentiated masses, so you can have as much of that as you are willing to handle. The fast-rising stars are those who question authority and refuse to do what's been done before.

The very system that is always looking for new talent, new ideas, and new approaches is only too happy to sap all the energy out of those that can be persuaded to work at the bottom of the pyramid.

WHEN EVERYTHING IS FREE

Washington, D.C., April 2010 — (AP) Spiraling price competition from China, India, Wal-mart, and Internet programmers is driving prices down to their lowest levels in one hundred years, the U.S. Commerce Department said yesterday.

Based on data it has collected, the Commerce Department issued an extraordinary warning: U.S. businesses should consider changing their business models to a donation-based system or face highly uncertain prospects, including Chapter 7 bankruptcy. In a related story, bankruptcy filings reached record levels last week . . .

Right now, the article above is a science-fiction story. Maybe a really bad one. But imagine if price competition played out to its ultimate end: Everything is free.

Or virtually free.

What if your company's business model was like that of public broadcasting?

That is, all of your products are free. You only earn revenue by convincing customers to donate money that represents their value of your product.

More than one thousand public radio and television stations in the United States operate this way every year. Many public broadcasters thrive, too. Average public-radio-station revenue is at its highest levels in years. National Public Radio is the fastest-growing radio format. In her will, Joan Kroc, a loyal NPR listener, left NPR $200 million when she died in 2003. It's not just the rich patrons that care, though. More than 25,000 people were so upset with a personality change on NPR that they signed an on-line petition within days. To get 25,000 people to sign *anything* is a feat in itself. Passionate attachment to public broadcasting is at an all-time high, supplemented by monetary donations and the volunteerism of customers who keep public broadcasters on the air.

A public-broadcasting business model could be creeping up on your company faster than you care to imagine or admit.

Severe price pressure is a growing reality for manufacturers of furniture, software, and electronics, as well as providers of call centers, accounting, and other white-collar jobs that can be accomplished by anyone with enough training. Perhaps a public-broadcasting business model isn't such a far-fetched scenario after all. A model that relies on donations and is based on free seems alien, but maybe that's the best route for the future of your organization.

For a moment, imagine that within a year global competition causes your company to rely on donations to survive. How will you prepare? How will you change your relationship with customers? Will you change at all?

Will you begin to treat customers like family? Will you involve them in the business, as many family-owned businesses do?

How will you attract and keep customers who will chip in extra money if you can't meet your yearly revenue goals?

How will you change your product to become so valuable that customers will pay a fair price after they've used it freely for a year?

What will you do differently to survive?

TUESDAYS WITH SHECKY: A PLAY IN THREE JOKES

(*The curtain rises. We're inside the Home for Retired Funnymen, an assisted-living facility for comics in their sunset years. Sitting in a La-Z-Boy chair, staring out the window at the Catskill Mountains, is UNCLE SHECKY. He's wearing a tattered robe and chewing on a cigar. Rushing into UNCLE SHECKY's room is his nephew, BEN.*)

                    BEN
              (*out of breath*)
    Uncle Shecky, what's wrong? I got
    your call and came over immediately.

                    UNCLE SHECKY
    Ben, my boy, I don't have much time
    left. So I've decided to let you in
    on some wisdom—to convey to you the
    lessons of my life and teach you the
    three secrets of being remarkable.
    Listen carefully.

                    BEN
        (*surprised and slightly awed*)
    I'm all ears.

                    UNCLE SHECKY
    Yes, I've noticed that since you
    were a child, Ben. You know, your
    cousin Jerry is a very well known
    plastic surgeon. He does excellent

work. He could help. But I digress.
Ben, there are three secrets to
being remarkable.

> BEN

What are they?

> UNCLE SHECKY

A guy walks into a doctor's office.
He says, "Doctor, it hurts when I do
this." And the doctor says . . .
Ben, what does the doctor say?

> BEN

"Don't do that."

> UNCLE SHECKY

Exactly! Now to the next secret. A
guy is walking to work one day and
right outside his office he sees a
penguin. He's startled, doesn't know
what to do. So he takes the penguin
into his boss's office and asks his
boss, "What should I do with this
penguin?" The boss looks at him and
says, "Take him to the zoo, you
idiot!" A few days later, out on the
street, the boss runs into the guy
and he still has the penguin. The
boss is shocked. He looks at the guy
and says, "I thought I told you to
take the penguin to the zoo!" And
the guy looks at his boss and
says . . .

(a pause as UNCLE SHECKY waits)

> BEN

"I did. But we had such a great
time, today I'm taking him to a ball
game."

> UNCLE SHECKY

Precisely! Oh, Ben, I'm so proud.

> BEN

Thank you, Uncle Shecky.

UNCLE SHECKY

Now the last secret. A woman from Ohio is walking in midtown Manhattan. She's a bit lost. She sees a man carrying a violin case, walks up to him, and asks him, "Excuse me, sir, how do you get to Carnegie Hall?" The violinist looks at her and says . . .

BEN

(*not waiting for the prompt*)
"Practice, practice, practice."

UNCLE SHECKY

Right! And those are the secrets to being remarkable.

BEN

Uh, I don't get it.

UNCLE SHECKY

Stop doing things that hurt; do what you love. Ignore what authority figures tell you. And most of all . . .

BEN

Practice, practice, practice.

UNCLE SHECKY

That's right, Ben.

(*UNCLE SHECKY clutches his chest.*)

UNCLE SHECKY
(*in a weak voice*)
You've been a great audience . . .

BEN

Uncle Shecky?

UNCLE SHECKY
(*his voice weaker still*)
Thank you . . . Good night . . .
Drive safely.

(*The curtain falls.*)

REAL ARTISTS SHIP

Steve Jobs was making a point—there's a difference between being a dilettante and acting in a way that actually makes a difference.

All-star designer Isaac Mizrahi says, "I used to think my job was about coming up with a new, bold, crazy look every six months, making something fabulous and pretty for my friends and the models." No longer. Today, Mizrahi gets excited when a retailer sells out. "I did this blended-wool toggle coat with a pink quilted lining for fifty dollars and Target sold something like seventeen thousand of them!"

It's awfully tempting to embrace the role of impatient outsider. It's fun to be the big thinker who is always dueling with the bureaucracy, bitter that your best ideas always get turned down or ruined by management. After all, you can't be criticized for ideas that never see the light of day. You can remain the secret genius you think you are.

You even see this in politics, where some pundits run away

from an idea as soon as it is about to be embraced by the majority. Technology, though, is where you'll find the Don Quixote syndrome the most often.

Here's an actual headline from the Web: REALNETWORKS HELIX PLAYER FOR LINUX: NOW WITH OGG VORBIS AND OGG THEORA

Ogg Vorbis is an open-source alternative to the MP3 format for music online. Linux is an alternative to Windows. And the RealNetworks player is an alternative to those made by Microsoft and Apple.

It's easy to argue that Linux is cheaper, faster, more reliable, and a worthy alternative to the Microsoft monopoly. But does the MP3 format really need a competitor? Most players don't support the open-source Ogg Vorbis format, hence most music isn't available in it. And the benefits to the user are slight at best. Yet there are thousands of Ogg Vorbis diehards out there, arguing the finer points of their open-source alternative.

The hard part, it seems, is figuring out when to fight and when to switch sides. When is it worth giving up perfection and compromising just to get something shipped? When is good enough *actually* good enough?

THIS IS YOUR FIRST TEST

You probably don't remember the first test you took. You didn't study and there wasn't a private prep class for it. You were one minute old. No number-two pencils, no fancy equipment. Just five simple observations recorded by a doctor. It's possible this test even saved your life.

This test is now commonly known as the Apgar score, an easy and objective method for evaluating a newborn's health just moments after birth. It is simple, noninvasive and has saved innumerable infants' lives around the world.

Virginia Apgar was a medical maverick. She was one of the first women ever to graduate with an M.D. from Columbia University, in 1933. In 1939 she became the first woman to head a department at Columbia University's College of Physicians and Surgeons, and in 1949 she became the first woman to be granted a full professorship in anesthesiology at the university.

As a result of the post–World War II baby boom and a social shift away from home births, significantly more babies were now being delivered in hospitals. Originally, a baby would be born, quickly cleaned, swaddled, and sent off to the nursery. It was assumed that an infant was in good health unless obvious symptoms of illness were visible. As a result, many respiratory or circulatory problems were not detected. Many infant deaths could have been prevented had there been a method for diagnosing a newborn's health.

After years of evaluating newborns soon after their births during her research as a perinatal anesthesiologist, Dr. Apgar wrote, "Birth is the most hazardous time of life." In response, she created a simple yet accurate assessment tool for evaluating a baby's health during the crucial minutes after birth, when diagnosis and intervention could help save its life. This "Newborn Scoring System" is now the international standard for evaluating a baby at birth.

The Newborn Scoring System assigns a maximum score of 2 points each to five criteria: heart rate, respiratory rate, reflex irritability (response to physical stimulation), muscle tone, and color. Assessment of each of these criteria is made twice, at one and five minutes after birth. A score of at least 7 on both assessments indicates a high likelihood of a healthy baby. Lower scores indicate problems that need to be diagnosed and, if necessary, treated immediately. To further simplify this evaluation, the acronym "APGAR" was developed by another physician to make the five criteria easier to learn and remember. The Apgar score, as the test is now commonly referred to, stands for (A) appearance; (P) Pulse; (G) grimace; (A) activity; (R) respiratory.

As a colleague of Apgar's observed, "Every baby born in a modern hospital anywhere in the world is now looked at first through the eyes of Virginia Apgar." The Apgar score has made a worldwide impact on saving babies' lives. It costs nothing, is simple to teach, and requires no complex technology. It took a lot of experience and common sense to create something so simple and streamlined. Yet the Apgar score has changed the world of perinatal care. No marketing budget, no technology, no charge. Just profound worldwide impact.

Sometimes you find remarkable innovations in the places you least expect.

ISAAC NEWTON'S HEAD

Ask any elementary-school kid about Isaac Newton and you'll hear the same answer: "He invented gravity!"

Of course, Newton did no such thing. Newton certainly invented calculus. He also invented the reflecting telescope. He did not invent the Fig Newton, though. That was Charles M. Roser.

Newton gets credit for inventing gravity because of a tree in his backyard. He was sitting in his garden, thinking about the moon, when he looked up and noticed that an apple on the tree nearby was precisely the same size (to his eye) as the moon. As an object gets farther away, it appears to be smaller. In a flash, Newton realized that the apple was proportional to the moon in size, and the effect of "gravitas" on each must be proportional as well. Newton had figured out that gravity decreased over distance. More important to his reputation, he gave gravity its name. The apple never actually hit him on the head, but the term "gravity" stuck.

While Newton spent far more time on calculus and on alchemy, he's known for discovering gravity. Why?

Because he named it.

To the average person, Newton's contribution to science was a word. A word that described something that was already there, something that affected everyone, all the time. By naming gravity, he gave us power over it. He gave us a handle, which permitted both scientists and laypeople to talk about and interact with this mysterious force.

Organizations change when you give something a name. If it has a name, your peers can measure it. If it has a name, they can alter it. If it has a name, they can talk about it. And if it has a name, they can eliminate it.

Go ahead, name something. (Watch your head!)

WHAT DO YOU STAND FOR?

Twenty years ago, Bruce Katz created shoes that were great for walking. What's new about that? Aren't all shoes great for walking?

In the early eighties, a trip to the shoe store would demonstrate that this certainly wasn't the case. There were street shoes, with thick leather soles and stiff uppers—the kind you laced up and wore to work. And then there were nylon running shoes that were lightweight and comfortable. You could be comfortable in them, but you couldn't wear them to work or on a date.

Katz, a young entrepreneur who craved comfort in everything he wore, married the two categories and created a new kind of footwear—walking shoes. Called Rockports, these shoes had thick yet lightweight soles, soft uppers, and high-tech comfort liners that hugged and soothed the foot.

The industry scoffed at his big idea. They didn't believe that consumers would go for his untraditional footwear. But Bruce believed that once people knew about the shoes, they'd buy them. His problem? Few marketing resources.

His pitch was simple: "They're great for walking," he would tell anyone who would listen.

Yet walking was something for old people. Young, hip people didn't walk. Men certainly didn't walk. There was no cachet to walking. No walking clubs, contests, events, clothes, or badges of achievement. And certainly no "walking lifestyle."

The insight that made people care about walking was to relate it to something they *did* care about—health. Within three years of the launch of Rockport, all of America was abuzz with talk about walking for health and fitness.

Health evangelist Rob Sweetgall walked 11,208 miles, traversing fifty states in fifty weeks, telling anyone who would listen: "Don't smoke, eat properly and walk." He walked alone, traveling the equivalent of a marathon a day, cushioned by three battered pairs of Rockports.

With Rockport's help, one book, a film, and thousands of articles later, millions of Americans were turned on to walking for health and fitness. Rockport had discovered the wisdom of standing for something worthwhile.

The company created the Rockport Walking Institute, a Rockport Fitness Test, and the Rockport Walking Diet, all scientifically validated. They freely shared information with thousands of health and walking advocates across the country. The fitness-walking movement was born, with Rockport leading the way.

In five years, Rockport increased in size 1000 percent, and earned more than $200 million in annual revenue.

Today, brands don't have much of a choice. They can either stand for something big and important to their consumers, or they can risk being categorized as trivial.

When Avon takes on breast cancer or LensCrafters embraces the fight for sight, they are transcending brand expectations and doing something worth doing, something that allows them to make a difference. IBM's commitment to education is bigger than anything their R&D or advertising groups can invent.

These companies have deep and sincere commitments to causes they believe in, and they manage those commitments the way they'd treat any other critical business asset.

In taking up worthwhile causes, brands stick their necks out for something greater and far more purposeful than their everyday work, and in return build brand relevance, organizational ethos and pride, and consumer preference and trust. And the world becomes just a little brighter and better.

Stand for something or stand for nothing.

HOW TO MAKE MONEY WITH GARLIC

Gilroy, California, is the garlic capital of the world. The town holds an annual garlic festival (serving delights like garlic ice cream) and grows the bulk of the garlic eaten in the United States.

Except they don't.

Even Gilroy's biggest garlic company, Christopher Ranch, is now selling garlic imported from China. It turns out that overfarming and commoditization have made growing garlic in Gilroy a poor bet. In the last five years, the value of Gilroy garlic sold in the market is down more than $70 million, while Chinese garlic sales are up 5000 percent.

At the same time that the California garlic outlook is becoming stinky, the more unusual hard-neck garlic crop from New York is thriving. It's harder to plant and harder to harvest, but many chefs and cooks believe that New York garlic is worth seeking out. Top restaurants in New York City and around the country pay a premium because the taste is worth it.

As soon as Gilroy garlic became the standard—sold far and wide because it was cheap and boring—the farmers in Gilroy opened themselves up to brutal price competition and gave in to the temptation of overplanting. *Once you make the standard, you've created a commodity.* Your customers will seek out stuff that's the same as yours, but cheaper. That's why China won.

The average New York garlic farm is a tiny fraction of the size of a California megafarm. Yet the New York farms are profitable and growing. Stan Erkson of Fort Plain Farm is one of the 265 New York garlic farmers (up from just a few in 1992) who are delighted that people are paying between five and nine dollars a pound for their rare and expensive garlic. He sold more than two thousand pounds worth in just a weekend—and some of that probably went into ice cream.

Was it inevitable that this brutal price competition would decimate Gilroy? Almost every industry moves toward commoditization. Customers in your industry (and every other) encourage producers to take incremental steps toward lower prices, dependable output, and homogenization. The problem, of course, is that once you're a commodity, you lose. In the short run, listening to the buyers and becoming boring can be profitable. In the long run, though, doesn't it make sense to ignore your customers and stay remarkable instead?

BE LIKE REGGIE

Reggie fixes bikes in Mt. Kisco, New York. For every bike he fixes (he charges by the hour and even a small job takes an hour) he does his best. Then he spends five extra minutes doing something special.

During that first hour, Reggie is a perfectly fine bike mechanic. He pays attention to detail and follows established protocol. He is careful and focused and diligent. Like one thousand other very good bike mechanics, he gets the job done and earns his pay.

In the last five minutes, though, Reggie transforms himself from a workman into an artist. In those few extra minutes, he becomes remarkable.

Sometimes, all he does is carefully clean the chain. Other times, he'll take the bike out to the potholed parking lot and be sure that the gears are adjusted properly. And sometimes, especially if the bike is for a cute kid, he'll attach a horn or some tassels—anything worth noticing.

The astonishing thing isn't how unusual Reggie is. The astonishing thing is how easy it is to do what Reggie does, and how many people *don't* do it. It doesn't matter if you're doing accounts payable or product design. Those last five minutes make it easy for your customers to find the difference between you and everyone else.

It takes 99 percent of the time you spend just to be average. The remarkable stuff can happen in a flash.

WHY NOT? WHY NOW?

A few questions to ask yourself:

What if we did things the way our competition did them?

What if we ended up on the endcap at Wal-Mart?

What if paper was free?

What if packaging cost ten times what it costs now?

What if we had to pay to dispose of anything our customers threw away?

What if we could charge ten times as much for this?

What if we had to charge one-tenth as much?

What if the instructions couldn't include illustrations?

If we were on *Oprah*, what would she say about us?

Why can't they make this in China for 30 percent of our costs?

Is it generous?

If the CEO loved this, how fast could we get it done?

Couldn't we do it just a little faster than that?

ARE YOU ALWAYS RUNNING OUT OF TIME?

On our way to a brainstorming meeting, a colleague turned to me and said, "I wish I had more time to prepare for this—I've been so busy I didn't do a thing for the meeting."

Busy? Doing what?

Just for fun, we made a diary of her workweek. She spends about forty-four hours a week at work, with four hours spent at lunch and stuff. So figure 2,400 minutes a week.

In a typical week, she spends 2,000 minutes playing defense—filling out forms, answering urgent requests, returning calls, and putting out fires. This is what most office workers refer to when they talk about "work."

She spends about 300 minutes in meetings, listening to other people talk about what they're going to do or have recently done.

She spends about 45 minutes actually doing creative work on the projects she's currently involved in.

And she spends exactly 15 minutes a week on inventing the next breakthrough.

This is scary stuff. Scary because if you do the math of what her organization actually gets paid for, it's precisely the opposite of the way my colleague spends her time. When she goes on vacation, those 2,000 minutes of urgent emergencies just sit there, and nothing particularly horrible happens. And in a rare week when she doubles her big-thinking time from 15 minutes to 30, she's likely to come up with a big moo—an insight that will pay the company's bills for the next six months or a year.

So, do you really think you're too busy to work on something remarkable? In fact, you're actually too busy to do all that (non-urgent) emergency stuff.

"BUT" OR "AND"?

How often do you say "yes, but"? At Sarah Lee, the top people walk around wearing white buttons with a big black slash through them. Those buttons prohibit anyone from saying the word "but."

What if you had to say "Yes, thanks!" or "Sure, how?" every time someone had a suggestion?

PANIC AT
INAPPROPRIATE TIMES

Panicking when something really bad happens is counter-productive.

The new Home Depot just down the street is having its grand opening sale—this is not the time to figure out a new strategy for your hardware store. It's way too late for that.

Imagine a potbellied, nervous, cigarette-smoking salesman, pacing back and forth in front of his office building. He's annoyed to be outside, but they won't let him smoke inside. He's puffing as hard as he can, anxious about getting back to work.

This guy is focused on solving the urgent problems in his life. And all those problems are about *today*. He's not focused one bit on losing weight or giving up cigarettes or understanding how tense he is. He figures that there will be time for that later.

Right now, he needs to panic about the sales numbers that are due tomorrow. He'll have time to panic about his health when he's in the hospital having bypass surgery.

The time to panic about his health is right now, of course,

while he can still do something about it. Taking action *today* on a long-term problem is easier, cheaper, more effective, and far less time consuming than waiting for it to become an emergency. The time to panic about his health is today. The time to panic about the sales numbers was last week.

Why not start panicking in advance? Why not start taking emergency measures while there's still a chance that those emergency measures will actually *accomplish* something?

Is your flagship product going to be obsolete in five years? You betcha. That means the time to start panicking about a replacement is right now, not in four years.

Every organization that gets into trouble falters because it waited too long to do the stuff that should have been done a long time ago. Panic early, not late, and your fire drills will actually pay off.

TEAR DOWN THIS WALL

Suppose that I had asked you, in the mid-1980s, what you thought it would take to bring down the Berlin Wall? What would you have said? I can imagine the answer. Perhaps another world war. Perhaps some kind of multilateral, long-term rapprochement between East and West Germany. At the very least, some kind of intervention costing many billions of dollars. Certainly that's the kind of scenario that was envisioned by all of the world's so-called experts on Eastern Europe. When it came to predicting the life span of the Soviet Bloc, the CIA, State Department, and Pentagon did not think in terms of months or even years. They thought in terms of decades.

But what actually happened? In September 1989, a small group of dissidents in Leipzig, East Germany, held a protest rally and—for reasons no one quite understands—the local police did not shut it down. The next day, in the next town over, another group of dissidents held a protest of their own, and it was a little bigger this time because they were emboldened by what happened in Leipzig. The police in that town didn't stop the protesters because, after seeing what happened in Leipzig, they thought that maybe they weren't supposed to do anything. The day after that, there was still another protest in the next town over—a little bit bigger than the last, the police a little more passive—and on and on. All through East Germany, the protests got bigger and bigger and the police grew more and more passive until a million people gathered in the streets of East Berlin in October 1989 and tore down the Berlin Wall as the police sat and watched.

This was the biggest change any of us will probably ever see in our lifetime. It took a month, it cost nothing, and it started with a handful of people in a town no one would ever have pegged as the birthplace of a revolution.

Remember that the next time someone says, "It can't be done."

THEY SAY I'M EXTREME

They say I'm extreme.
I say I'm a realist.

They say I demand too much.
I say they accept mediocrity and continuous improvement too readily.

They say, "We can't handle this much change."
I say, "Your job and career are in jeopardy; what other options do you have?"

They say, "What's wrong with a 'good product'?"
I say, "Wal-Mart or China or both are about to eat your lunch. Why can't you provide instead a fabulous experience?"

They say, "Take a deep breath. Be calm."
I say, "Tell it to Wal-Mart. Tell it to China. Tell it to India. Tell it to Dell. Tell it to Microsoft."

They say the Web is a useful tool.
I say the Web changes everything. Now.

They say, "We need an initiative."
I say, "We need a dream. And dreamers."

They say great design is "nice."
I say great design is necessary.

They say, "Effective governance is important."
I say bold, brash boards that are representative of the market served—more than a token woman or two and an empty seat for the "forthcoming Hispanic"—are an imperative. Now.

They say, "Plan it."
I say, "Do it."

They say, "We need more steady, loyal employees."
I say, "We need more 'freaks' who routinely tell those in charge to take a flying leap . . . before it's too late."

They say, "We need Good People."
I say, "We need Quirky Talent."

They say, "We like people who, with steely determination, say, 'I can make it better.'"
I say, "I love people who, with a certain maniacal gleam in their eye, perhaps even a giggle, say, 'I can turn the world upside down. Watch me!'"

They say, "Sure, we need change."
I say we need *revolution now*.

They say, "Fast follower."
I say, "Battered and bruised leader."

They say, "Conglomerate and imitate!"
I say, "Create and innovate!"

They say, "Market share."
I say, "Market creation."

They say, "Improve and maintain."
I say, "Destroy and reimagine."

They say, "Normal."
I say, "Weird."

They say, "Happy balance."
I say, "Creative tension."

They say they favor a "team that works and lives in harmony."
I say, "Give me a raucous brawl among the most creative people imaginable."

They say, "Peace, brother."
I say, "Bruise my feelings. Flatten my ego. *Save my job*."

They say, "Basic black."
I say, "Technicolor rules!"

They say, "We need happy customers."
I say, "Give me pushy, needy, nasty, provocative customers."

They say, "We seek Harvard M.B.A.s."
I say, "I seek certificate-free 'Ph.D.s' from the School of Hard Knocks."

They say they want recruits with "spotless records."
I say, "The spots are what matter most."

They say, "Integrity is important."
I say, "Tell the unvarnished truth, all the time . . . or take a hike."

They say diversity is a "good thing."
I say diversity is a breath of fresh, creative air—absolutely necessary for economic salvation in perilous times.

They say it's "daunting."
I say it's "a hoot."

They say, "Zero defects."
I say, "A day without a screwup or two is a day pissed away."

They say, "Think about it."
I say, "Try it."

They say, "Plan it."
I say, "Test it."

They say, "Radical change takes a decade."
I say, "Radical change takes a minute."

They say, "Times are changing."
I say, "Everything has already changed. Tomorrow is the first day of your revolution . . . or you're toast."

They say, "We can't all be revolutionaries."
I say, "Why not?"

They say, "We can't all be a brand."
I say, "Why not?"

They say this is just a rant.
I say this is just reality.

THE REMARKABLE GERTRUDE BELL

Gertrude Bell was born in Victorian England in 1868 and raised in the shadow of England's greatest role model of the time, Queen Victoria. Her life was meant to be conventional. Her parents' aspirations were for her to become "a good wife, a good mother, and a good woman." Incredibly bright, honest, and assertively forthright (not necessarily the most desired qualities for a Victorian lady), she grew up to become one of the most powerful people in the British Empire.

Gertrude was the first woman in the history of Oxford University to receive First Class honors in modern history. She traveled the world extensively, circumnavigating the globe twice. She was a brilliant fencer and an avid mountain climber. In fact, she was one of the first women to climb the Engelhorn in Switzerland.

At the age of twenty-three she traveled to Persia, where she quickly immersed herself in the culture, the history, and the politics of the Arab world. She learned to speak fluent Persian, studied cultural anthropology, and traveled extensively into the desert, befriending the sheikhs of various nomadic tribes and making several important archaeological discoveries.

As World War I approached, her firsthand knowledge of the Middle East earned her service with the British Intelligence. In 1915 she was appointed to the Arab Bureau in Cairo. She was also part of the Mesopotamia Expeditionary Force in Basra and Baghdad.

Winston Churchill broke with all convention and appointed her oriental secretary to the British High Commission in Iraq. In 1921 he summoned the greatest experts on the Middle East to a conference in Cairo to determine the future of Mesopotamia (Iran and Iraq). There were thirty-nine men at this conference (including Lawrence of Arabia) and one woman: Gertrude Bell.

It's fair to say that Gertrude didn't start out with a specific goal or objective. She didn't plan to become an expert on the Arab world. She found her purpose by nurturing her thirst for knowledge and adventure. Her passion and defiant independence set her on a remarkable course of unparalleled achievement for a woman of her era.

The New York Times once remarked about Gertrude: "The ways of English women are strange. They are probably the greatest slaves to conventionality in the world, but when they break with it, they do it with a vengeance."

It takes courage to do what you want. A lot of other people have a lot of other plans for you.

Gertrude Bell became the Desert Queen precisely because she broke with convention and followed her heart with a vengeance.

That's what remarkable leaders do.

THREE STEPS AHEAD

One step is easy. One step isn't enough. If you're only one step ahead, by the time your organization gets done working on your idea, it'll be too late. Big organizations with lots of power fall in love with one-step innovations. They believe that their power will be enough to defeat the competition by the time they get to market. And sometimes they're right.

Two steps is tempting. Two steps means that everyone understands what you're up to when you pitch an idea to them. Two steps means that you can get funded or approved by a visionary organization. But two steps is still a problem, because your smart competitors are three steps ahead. Your organization will ultimately be defeated by the competitors that are willing to take three steps.

Three steps changes the game. Organizations that think three steps ahead are the groundbreakers and the pathfinders. They're the ones inventing the next generation, the people who are undoing the very foundations that your organization depends on.

Three steps is difficult. It's difficult to sell, even more difficult to build, and almost impossible to get your mother-in-law (or your boss) to understand. Three steps—that's what's worth building.

MR. BUTT'S SHOPPERS

Wal-Mart may have its 1,600 supercenters and its low, low prices, but Charles E. Butt of H-E-B Grocery Company (www.heb.com) has a culture of restless dissatisfaction and a relentless focus on thinking like his shoppers. That makes him and his 304 stores and $11 billion in annual sales a force to be reckoned with in the Lone Star State, reports Susan Warren in *The Wall Street Journal.* Just to give you an idea of how Mr. Butt's culture thinks about its shoppers, H-E-B's president of food and drugs, Suzanne Wade, once handed twenty dollars to several employees and told them to feed a family of four for a week. She comments: "We found out why beans and rice and tortillas sell so well." In another example, managers in the Rio Grande valley, noticing an annual spike in rubbing alcohol sales, discovered it was because customers who couldn't afford air-conditioning were using the alcohol to cool their skin.

Problem was, regular alcohol dries the skin, so H-E-B worked with manufacturers to develop its own brand of rubbing alcohol with moisturizers, which now makes up a quarter of its rubbing alcohol sales. Sometimes such insight simply takes the form of novelty, such as their hot-selling Texas-shaped tortilla chips. Other times it determines product assortment, such as stocking barbecue grill "discos" favored by Mexican Americans in southern-border stores, and traditional gas grills used by Anglos elsewhere around Texas. Mr. Butt even installed live tanks of fish and shellfish in a southwest Houston store that caters to Asians. He imported a spiny Asian fruit called durian after one of his executives noticed a long line forming for the peculiar fruit at a food market in Thailand. Perhaps most interesting of all, Mr. Butt's fixation on understanding how his shoppers think ultimately takes square aim at Wal-Mart's claim to fame—low prices.

Specifically, at his downtown Houston store, produce is priced by the piece, instead of by the pound, because that results in better sales from buyers who come in with just twenty dollars in their hands. The thing about Wal-Mart, says H-E-B Houston's Scott McClelland, is that "it forces you to be better."

WHAT, EXACTLY, ARE YOU AFRAID OF?

Here's a list. You pick:

- getting yelled at by the boss
- getting fired
- having your company close down for lack of business
- your company gets acquired and you get fired
- not getting promoted
- making promises you can't keep
- doing the wrong thing
- getting caught using the copy machine after hours
- not knowing the right answer

Here's the big news: If your strategy is to lie low, do your job, follow instructions, and hope that nobody notices you, (a) nobody *will* ever notice you, and (b) you're actually increasing the chances of something bad happening.

If, on the other hand, you develop a reputation as the person who is always pushing the envelope, challenging the organization to go to the next level, and using your influence to get good stuff done, you've got the world's best job security. If you never pretend to know all the answers, nobody will hate you when you say, "I don't know." And if you surround yourself with a team that depends on you to lead them to the next big thing, you all benefit.

You can't shrink your way to greatness.

THE ONE THING YOU
CAN'T DOWNLOAD

Brian Camelio had a problem. The Internet was making it impossible to make money selling records.

What Brian realized was that anyone could download music for free. Dozens of industries, including the music business, are threatened by technology, and the usual response is to fret or to sue. Brian did neither. Instead, he realized that free downloads could be an asset—as long as he could figure out something to sell that would benefit from the viral nature of downloading. He realized that one thing that couldn't be downloaded was the creative process itself. His concept, then, was to try to capture that process and sell it.

As Brian articulates on his Web site, www.ArtistShare.com, a recorded song is like a snapshot, a moment in time along a creative continuum. That continuum, says Brian, is a living, breathing thing. So why limit music fans to just the part that's on the CD?

The bigger opportunity was to allow fans to come along for the entire creative ride. So, in addition to selling music CDs for

$16.95, ArtistShare also invites fans to purchase anything and everything that surrounds the making of the music.

Take jazz composer Maria Schneider, for example. Maria began her career as a solo artist with both a dedicated following and enough of her own money to make her own recording. What she had never seen was a profit from any of her records . . . until she sold and marketed her music the Brian Camelio way.

Indeed, on ArtistShare.com, Maria's fans spent an average of fifty-three dollars—that's nearly three times the price of her CD—on the context of her creativity. They spent it on things like music scores, videos of rehearsal sessions, interviews, and tutorials. But they're also spending fifty-three dollars to feel like patrons of the arts, like people who can support the creative work of others. Not only has Maria actually made money on one of her records through ArtistShare, but she almost certainly has tightened the bond with her fans along the way.

Jazz guitarist Jim Hall is also making money with ArtistShare, and Brian says he's signed a whole bunch of other artists, including Danilo Pérez, Dave Holland, Brian Lynch, Monday Michiru, David Binney, and Deanna Witkowski. He's also about to announce a project with Trey Anastasio, formerly of Phish, who says that ArtistShare is "quite possibly the future of the music industry."

Of course, you're not in the music business. Your business is different, because . . . because . . . actually, it's not different at all. When technology threatens the model you've come to depend on, whining is rarely a viable solution. Turning the business upside down is a lot more productive.

THE BELL CURVE

Some people are always in the middle of the bell curve.

Take any population anywhere on the planet and measure just about anything, and the distribution of the population almost always comes out as a perfect bell curve. Weird? No. Just very normal.

Take height, for example. There are a few Willie Shoemakers and a few Kareem Abdul-Jabbars, but just about everyone is grouped in the middle.

It's one thing to be physically average, but the bell curve also applies to effort, attitude, and skill. It even applies to the energy and creativity of entire organizations. There are a few at each end of the curve, but most organizations end up in the middle.

Did these people and organizations *choose* to be average, or did it just end up that way?

We know that in just about any marketplace, the laggards get wiped out. Organizations that lag behind the competition's new products see their sales decline. Individuals who don't exert enough energy are more likely to get laid off.

The most fascinating thing about the bell curve is that some people and some organizations naturally gravitate to a certain section. Some people, for example, will always walk a few steps behind the group, regardless of how fast the group is walking. Some companies will always fill their orders a little faster than everyone else, regardless of the industry average.

The trick, then, is not to wait for your industry to change before changing where you are on the curve. The trick is to change your organization's instinctual location on the curve. If you get used to being exceptional, you'll probably stay there.

FEAR VERSUS ANXIETY

Quick! There's an enraged tiger loose in the office. *Run!* Can you feel yourself running as fast as you possibly can? Heart pounding, taking the corners at top speed, slipping on the carpet, knocking over the watercooler?

That's fear. Fear is a good thing.

Fear saves our lives in the jungle, in the streets, and even at the doctor's office. Fear is one of the most useful emotions you've got.

Anxiety, on the other hand, is a killer. Anxiety is the false fear that corrupts your life. Anxiety is what happens when you imagine possible negative outcomes instead of embracing the reality of right now.

Anxiety is also the reason that organizations overstudy opportunities—and then hesitate to take action until it's too late.

Make a list of the last fifteen things you and your peers were anxious about. How many of them actually occurred? If you had ignored that anxiety, wouldn't things have gone a lot more smoothly?

TOO RICH, TOO THIN . . . TOO EFFICIENT?

"When the rate of change outside exceeds the rate of change inside, *the end is in sight."*

—Jack Welch

In the summer of 2003, *The New York Times*'s business page top story led with "Ford Plant Finds Efficiency Is No Protector," reporting on the closing of the world's most efficient light-truck plant. It had been optimized to produce a model that, alas, was no longer in demand.

Two days later, on the same page, a story about a Honda plant, titled "Yes, Assembly Lines Can Mix Apples and Oranges," described a factory capable of making both Civics and Elements, insulating Honda against the need to anticipate the condition of the market. Efficiency, the holy grail of industrial design in a predictable world, was trumped by robustness—the ability to roll with the punches.

How can a business ensure robustness? There's a clue in the

U.S. Department of Agriculture's practice of keeping hundreds of strains of corn in reserve, in case some new blight or climatic condition turns up that affects the half-dozen or so strains that are in use. This ensures that our corn "factory" can withstand some disruption. Of course, there is an "inefficiency" involved: A few resources need to go into running the Department of Agriculture.

In an organization, the equivalent of stockpiling diverse strains is to increase the diversity of points of view within the enterprise. How could a company do this?

- *Create a group hiring criterion* by only hiring leaders who bring something new—be it an academic discipline, cultural experience, physical capability, hobby, family background, or language skill—to the team.
- *Cultivate the fringe* by finding out who disagrees with current directions, constructively or not, and harvest the diversity of opinion.
- *Cross-pollinate the ideas* that come from the first two strategies so that innovative combinations, rather than compromises, arise.

All of these measures reduce the efficiency of an organization as it is traditionally measured. Research has shown that teams that perform well on well-defined tasks tend to be homogeneous and to know each other well. The strategies above take a group in the opposite direction, toward heterogeneity. But when the game changes, monocultures don't have a repertoire of alternatives to draw on for new responses; like the dinosaurs, they lack the capacity to adapt.

At BP, adaptability isn't just organizational strategy—it's business strategy. Lord John Browne, BP's chairman, reasons that by creating an adaptive enterprise BP can make even unpredictable industry change a strategic ally. Blessed with a naturally diverse workforce as a consequence of doing business all over the world, BP makes concerted efforts to harvest and cross-pollinate the views of its employees. BP's confidence in its quick ability to respond occasionally leads the company to incite industry change, for example, by calling for tighter emissions standards. It may be costly for BP to adapt—but not as costly as they expect it to be for their competitors.

Efficiency is a good thing, but we measure it in too short a time frame, the traditional index of output per man-hour being an extreme example. Robustness looks to progress over a longer period. BP sees an industry shift toward cleaner energy, for example, and believes that the efficient way to get there is to make the first move, relying on an adaptive organization to make the adjustment.

In the 1970s, managers expanded the frame in which they evaluated costs to include a product's lifetime. In the 1980s, they expanded their view of quality to include the customer. Now it's time to expand our concept of efficiency to include the costs of adapting to changing business conditions—and the risks of failing to adapt.

"Giving up the illusion that you can predict the future is a very liberating moment. All you can do is give yourself the capacity to respond . . . the creation of that capacity is the purpose of strategy."

Lord John Browne

GET OUT!

Why do so many high-powered business meetings take place on the eighteenth hole of a world-class golf course or thirty thousand feet above the fairway in a richly appointed private jet? Because traditional executives love to demonstrate their mastery by dazzling colleagues, customers, and investors with their position and success.

The reality, though, is that in a world of disruptive innovation, where the premium is on continuous creativity, the enclaves of the corporate elite are more prisons than perks. They not only keep the rank and file (and all of their ideas) out, they keep leaders in (and closed off from a universe of opportunities to learn and grow).

There's a simple fix: Get out. Seriously, Get out! Get up from behind your desk and get out of your office.

This isn't about taking a vacation or "management by walking around."

This isn't about spending time on the shop floor, listening to your customers, or clocking the competition.

Those are all important activities, but they're not how the future is created. You have to go much further than that. If you want to do anything new in the marketplace, you've got to get as serious, rigorous, and creative about renewing yourself as any other aspect of your business. So, get out.

GET OUT OF YOUR COMFORT ZONE

You may be the master of your domain in your office, but chances are you're also a victim of your mastery. Too often in the business world, we preserve and revere experience when we should be challenging and renewing it. Go out and get some in-experience. Go back to square one. Put yourself in a position to discover something new. How? Send an invitation.

In 2004, advertising powerhouse Wieden+Kennedy launched a pioneering advertising school called "12" with a classified ad headlined: TALENTED/DIRECTIONLESS, WITH $/TIME TO SPARE?

Twelve lucky, brilliant misfits spent a year inside the agency. It's an ongoing experiment in inviting naïveté, passion, and new talent into the organization. The students learn advertising—and their teachers learn to see with fresh eyes.

Of course, you don't have to be young to think young. Schedule a playdate—with yourself. Pick up a new tool (video camera, paintbrush, spatula) and use it without an agenda. Try something you've never done before (plant a garden, give a speech) without judgment.

GET OUT OF YOUR FRAME OF REFERENCE

The best way to open your mind is to apply a jolt of unfamiliarity. Yes, this is hard for any grown-up, and especially tough if you live in the managerial bubble. That's why you have to make it a personal goal to seek out new sources, mix up your milieus, and rearrange your references. Go on a field trip. Go somewhere you've never been before: a skateboard park, a flea market, a town council meeting. Think contrast. If you live in the suburbs, spend an afternoon exploring a bustling, diverse metropolitan neighborhood. Think about engaging senses you rarely use. If your work is highly visual, go to a chamber music performance and close your eyes. Let your questions lead. If you're interested in honing your powers of observation, tour a forensics lab. Go out of your way. Build time for wandering into any trip. Watch a movie in a foreign language. Eat street food. Take public transportation.

GET OUT OF YOUR OWN SKIN

It's not enough to mix it up with the rich resources available out in the world—you also have to stir up the passions, dreams, and projects lying dormant inside yourself. We all lug around an accumulation of fantasy vocations and achievements. Pick one and start moonlighting. The head of strategy at a major design firm gave up her weekends (and kept up her fifty-hour workweeks) for eighteen months to complete a grueling degree at a top cooking school. Now her food fantasy is a real-life opportunity to work with one of the most celebrated chefs in the country. But following your fantasy doesn't have to mean stretching yourself thin or switching careers—it can mean jump-starting a project (authorized or not) that rewrites your job description. The most progressive organizations understand the value of cultivating these personal passions. Exhibit A: Google's policy of encouraging its brilliant engineers to spend 20 percent of their work time on projects of their own choosing (which often evolve into new features and product lines for the company).

None of these are extracurricular activities. *They're at the heart of growth.* Have you ever noticed that the most remarkable, fascinating, and successful people and companies don't actually work on becoming remarkable, fascinating, and successful? No, they spend their time and energy seeking out other remarkable, fascinating, and successful people, places, and experiences. Their curiosity is rivaled only by their humility. Their driving force is one of exploration: They're willing to risk discomfort, to ask unanswerable questions, to start over. The good news for all of us is that it's never too late for that. And it's as simple at this: Don't be a corporate shut-in, marking time until your time is up. The future is not lurking under your desk—it's outside.

So, get up and get out!

DON'T BE LIKE PETE

Pete runs a print shop. He's been in the same location for fifty-two years. He loves what he does and he's good at it.

All the local real estate agents, teachers, and businesspeople rave about Pete's place. He greets every customer—new and old—with a warm cup of freshly brewed coffee and a plate of chocolate-chip cookies. "Pete's a great guy," they all say.

"Never misses a deadline."

"Knows the printing business like the back of his hand."

"It's a pleasure to shoot the breeze with him."

No wonder Pete's been so successful all these years. He loves his customers, and his customers love him.

Two years ago, Pete decided it was time to expand. "Print on demand is just the thing to move us into the Internet age. We'll be just like Kinko's!" he declared.

One year and tens of thousands of dollars later, his new Web site went live. When customers called for appointments to see him, Pete gave them a Web address instead.

"You're gonna love it!" Pete told them. "Order what you want, whenever you want! Just like at Kinko's!"

Pete's customers weren't very happy. No more coffee. No more chats. No more chocolate-chip cookies.

A year after his new site went live, Pete the printer calls me to ask, "Hey, got any business to send my way?"

Pete's problem was that he wanted to be like someone else, when what made him remarkable in the first place was just being himself. Had Pete asked his customers about his idea first, he would have saved himself tens of thousands of dollars and dozens of longtime customers—not to mention their referrals.

Your customers are your best advisers. They'll tell you what you're doing right, what you're doing wrong, and what it is they want you to change, if anything. But you have to ask them first.

So please—don't be like Pete. Pick three of your very best customers. Call them this week. Ask them what you're doing right. What are you doing wrong? What can you do better? What else do they wish you would do? Tell them your biggest ideas about your company's future. Is it difficult? Of course it is. That first phone call will put a lump in your throat. Until you start to listen. You may be surprised, like Pete, to find that they love you just the way you are.

Being a remarkable company doesn't require spending tens of thousands or tens of millions on "reinvention." Customers sometimes love the simple stuff—having a human answer the phone on the first ring, receiving work ahead of time, learning new ways of approaching critical challenges, being connected with your other customers, and getting a special thank you reminding them that you value more than their business . . . you value their success.

TEN THINGS SMART
START-UPS KNOW

1. Failure Is an Option

When failure isn't an option, then there's no opportunity for experimentation or risk or growth. Start-ups that don't grow don't exist for long, so platitudes don't work. Instead, smart start-ups embrace smart failures as the only way to get to success.

2. Bravery Is Contagious

Yes, your boss may be a brave leader, valiantly risking everything in search of growth (and glory). Too often, though, big companies have too few brave leaders. By the time a company gets big, fear is much more common than bravery. The only way to find real success is for the entire team to challenge the status quo. Smart leaders spread the bravery around. When everyone is brave, it's a lot easier to change the world.

3. Invent the Market

Too often, established companies spend their time trying to pre-serve the status quo (the record industry is a great example). Smart start-ups try to make new markets instead. Combine the power of your organization with the desire to invent a new market and things will happen.

4. Customers Are Last (and First)

Customers are the last thing smart start-up employees think about when they go to bed and the first thing they think about at breakfast. It's not enough to just interview or visit with customers—especially if you want to keep them. The goal should be to find true intimacy, living with them until you get kicked out. Develop capabilities to monitor the differences between what you offer and what your customers/partners really want.

5. Rule Books Are Dispensable

Start-ups don't have the time to write a rule book. They do that *after* they've invented a new market. Why not throw your rule book out? What's the worst that could happen?

6. Lose the Slackers

"I stopped looking for work the day I found a job." If that's the of-ficial coffee cup mantra of your office, you've got troubles. A start-up is like a shallow stream—you can see the rocks at the bottom. Of course it's uncomfortable to confront those who stopped looking for work a long time ago—that's why most companies are stuck with who've they've got.

7. Grind Coffee, Not People

At a successful start-up, people are assets, not raw material. Smart investors know that it's great people that make an organization work, not patents or machines or locations. So start-ups do best when they organize a group of hypersmart, motivated people and give them a lot of coffee . . . but they lose when they burn their people out.

8. Test for Kool-Aid

Being cool is one thing, but if a start-up believes too much of its own hype, it's all over quickly. A new business can't afford to ignore feedback from the outside world. Conduct random Kool-Aid testing to keep egos in check, hierarchies small, company self-image honest, and real customer issues on everyone's priority list.

9. Always On

We're not closed, so why are you? The Web is always on, and so are your competitors.

10. Fire the CEO

Five years from now, all of a start-up's founding team will be in new jobs, and some of them will have left the organization.

Fast-growing organizations can't afford to guarantee that someone will be in a certain position forever. To grow, you have to make the tough calls and bring in the next level of talent, including (gasp) a new CEO.

GOTTA SERVE SOMEBODY

Shaun Considine rescued the greatest song in the history of rock and roll—from the trash.

In 1965, the VP of sales and marketing at Columbia Records took a look at Bob Dylan's new song, "Like a Rolling Stone." He didn't listen to it—he just looked at it and decided it was way too long to be released as a single. It would never get radio airplay and wouldn't sell, he said. Dylan refused to compromise the length. So, astonishingly, the master (one second short of six minutes in length) was thrown into the trash.

Shaun was working at Columbia at the time, as the coordinator of new releases. Shaun found the record—a studio-cut acetate—wrapped it up, took it home, and listened to it over the weekend.

As it happened, Shaun was part owner of a hot New York City club at the time, called Arthur, on East Fifty-fourth Street. This club was so hot that Dylan himself had been turned away (he showed up in "wine-stained, beer-splattered Army-Navy store couture"). Shaun slipped his copy of the song to the DJ, and the place went nuts, including two influential people who happened to be in the audience—a DJ from WABC and a programmer from WMCA, two of the most important stations in New York.

The two radio guys rang up Columbia and demanded copies of the song. Columbia complied—they even shipped it in red plastic to flag it as a hot record. Despite the conservative fears of the marketing department, the record was a hit.

If it weren't for Shaun, *Rolling Stone* magazine would never even have heard the song, and certainly wouldn't have chosen it as the number-one rock-and-roll song of all time.

Maybe you don't own a rock club. Maybe you don't know Bob Dylan. But you've still got as much power as Shaun Considine. What's in the trash that needs to see the light of day, needs to be run by a customer or tried out on a playground?

THE ORIGINALITY BUMP

Nothing is original. Most composers, great or not so great, are working with the same musical alphabet of pitches. It's putting the pitches together differently that creates something remarkable.

All artists want a new sound. Every time they sit down to compose, they are searching for a sound that speaks to them. And sooner or later, when they are far enough along in arranging and rearranging that set number of pitches, they try their "new sound" out on an audience. Not every audience will go for it, but sometimes it clicks. Eventually, every successful composer finds her niche.

Where does inspiration come from? Some folks think it comes from inside, from some little voice or spark of an idea. Some folks think it's an outside stimulus: a picture, a word, a smell, anything that gets them charged. Or focused in a way they had not been focused before.

Conversations can also be inspiring. Amazing ideas have

come from simple, innocent conversations. Conversations have led to ideas for airplanes, novels, buildings, even marketing strategies. Having someone to bounce ideas off of, to push them up against, is often the key. It's why so many great musical compositions have sprung up from teams of writers/composers.

After an idea is inspired, we must give it space and allow it to sprout. Then we nurture it until it blooms.

WHAT BUSINESS CAN
LEARN FROM DANCERS

Great artists are always looking to leave their mark. While some dancers are driven to become brilliant interpreters of others' work, they are not unique. Remarkable artists are always trying to find a way to put their own signature on their work. They try to tell their own story. They simply *can't* perform like everyone else. The message: Be like an artist. Better still, *be* an artist.

Jack Cole was a dance innovator who worked out of Hollywood. He was a mentor to many famous dancers. Uniquely, he incorporated East Indian dance into his style, taking it out of its pure form and jazzing it up. He'd add a shoulder roll, a flick of the finger. The dance became his.

Bob Fosse, a student of Cole's, took that style, put *his* own spin on it, and made it fly. An award-winning dancer, choreographer, and director for Broadway and film, Fosse was not known for his stellar dance technique. He was often accused of having "bad feet" (feet that turned in instead of out), terrible posture (he hunched, an absolute no-no for a dancer), and poor flexibility. But Fosse used his awkward, atypical style to his advantage. Instead of forcing himself into positions that were just too foreign for his body, he incorporated his bad habits into an original style that became his trademark. Instead of hiding who he was, he flaunted it, and Fosse's choreography became a landmark. Instead of pandering to others' expectations of style and form, he did something new.

Isadora Duncan wanted to move differently, to go beyond her classical-dance background. For her, the work needed to be different. So, she let her hair down, took off her clothes, and danced in a new style. Duncan had the ability to express her ideas with charisma, humor, pathos, and abandon. She took that bold leap and she succeeded. She broke away from the dance conventions of her day to emerge, virtually unchallenged, as the mother of modern dance.

José Limón was born in Culiacán, Mexico, in 1908. He was the eldest of twelve children. Dancing seemed miles away to someone with his background and upbringing. Even so, he had a need to break free from the restrictions he found in dance. Finding his inspiration from a modern-dance concert he attended as a young man, he chose to ignore the limitations of his background.

Limón didn't start dancing until his early twenties, pretty late for a professional dancer. He didn't have a dancer's body, either. Many said that he should not have been dancing at all. Even so, he was able to set the modern-dance field on its ear, becoming American modern dance's first male star. He was considered electric. He had a story to tell, and he danced his story. What's your story? What story are you waiting to tell?

None of these artists followed the form's artistic norms. They were the misfits and the oddballs. Each, in his or her own way, set out to do something brand-new and timeless, utilizing what was inherently unique inside. And each of them was uniquely qualified to do just that.

Just like you. No carbon copies allowed!

EVERYONE NEEDS A ROOF

Since 1980, plenty of people have come to Telluride, Colorado, seeking to make a fortune from a booming ski town. There are real-estate developers, ski area operators, fancy boutique owners, and even those who make a living by offering oxygen-rich hyperbaric chambers for wealthy, out-of-breath skiers.

Sometimes it seems as though the secret of remarkableness is to be glamorous or cutting-edge or fashionable. Matt Miles knows better.

In 1983, Matt learned how to put a roof on a house. He was working in central Texas and was about twenty years old. Miles moved back to Telluride and started a career as a remarkable roofer.

He offered nothing flashy, just first-rate roofing and a reputation for honesty and commitment. As a result of this remarkable mantra, Miles become the go-to roofer, the man to call whether you wanted a roof for a $10 million house or a renovated miner's shack.

Shingle by shingle, Matt has refused to compromise. As a result, he has bootstrapped his business to the point where he owns two trailer parks, a golf course, a prefab-house-manufacturing plant, and an 887-unit subdivision under development. Even better, he also has a seventy-two-acre tree farm where he grows the trees he uses to make his wood shingles.

In a marketplace filled with corner-cutting operators in a hurry, Matt Miles stands out for his steadfast refusal to be either corner-cutting or in a hurry.

WHERE DO IDEAS COME FROM?

Where do good—or, even better, *great*—ideas come from? Let's start with where they *don't* come from.

As the pace of change continues to increase, as competition becomes more unpredictable, as customers grow more powerful and find more options, the old sources of great ideas seem ill suited to the job of coming up with new ones.

You can't depend on great ideas coming from the Department of Great Ideas. Or from the R&D lab or the Innovation Department or from the Skunk Works. That's not to say that these operations should be shut down or dismissed. It's just that they aren't enough anymore. They can't do it alone.

You won't get the great ideas you need from the vice president of strategy or the head of new product development. They've got hurdle rates to consider, budgetary constraints to navigate, and lots of competing claims on their time, attention, and political support.

And you *definitely* can't wait for great ideas to come from the CEO. He or she may be at the top of the heap, but that doesn't mean a thing when it comes to generating the best thinking. By the time most CEOs actually make it to the top, they're running on intellectual fumes, having already spent their creativity in the jobs they had that propelled them to the top. It's been a long time since they read, saw, thought, or experienced anything fresh, new, or creative.

Enough bad news. Where do great ideas come from?

1. From New Hires Fresh, green recruits to your team, your division, your company, are about as far from the top as you can get (Think of the Tim Robbins character in *The Hudsucker Proxy,* showing up in the mail room with a great idea in his shoe.) The new hires in any organization are the first resource for generating great new ideas. Why? *Because they have fresh eyes.* They bring a clean slate to your world. The truth is, all of us have a tendency to become inured to the daily operations of the workplace. Small inconsistencies or inadequacies gradually become acceptable; opportunities for improvement or innovation go by the boards because we simply don't see them anymore. But new hires see them. They ask the simple but necessary questions: Why do we do it like that? Couldn't we do it better?

Suggestion: Do what entrepreneurial hotelier Chip Conley does at his Joie de Vivre properties. Make it a habit to sit down with your new hires at about the three-month point. But don't give them a performance review—ask them to give your operation a performance review. After three months, their eyes are still fresh enough that they'll be able to see things you're missing. And they'll have been on the job long enough to know how things really work. Chances are good that they'll have a few great ideas to contribute.

2. *From People on the Periphery* It used to be the case in most organizations that if you got transferred to a part of the company out in the boondocks your career was in trouble. These days, chances are good you'll finally have a chance to participate in some meaningful innovation. The reason is simple: In many companies, headquarters is the bastion of the status quo; the closer you get to the throne, the less of a chance you have to try new things. But out on the periphery, experimentation can take place. This is where new ideas are born, tested, tried, refined. If they work, they can always be repatriated to headquarters. If they fail, they can be given a quiet, dignified burial, and no one ever hears about those ideas again.

The landscape of great ideas is littered with winners that started out on the periphery and gradually made it back to headquarters: The Boston Consulting Group's wildly successful time-based competition strategy came from smart observers in Japan, but really took off when it came back to the United States. Levi's Dockers began in South America, then became all the rage in the middle-aged, slightly paunchy men's market in the United States. If you're looking for good ideas—or you want a better shot at generating some yourself—move to the periphery. It's where the action is.

3. *From Front-Line Workers* The best ideas often come from the people with the dirtiest fingernails. They're the tech reps at Xerox who actually repair the machines, and can offer the engineers and product development people a bundle of ways to make their products better and more reliable, if anybody cared to listen. They're the call service reps who actually talk—and even more important, listen—to customers. Almost every company will tell you that the voice of the customer needs to be heeded—and the call service folks are the ones who have it ringing in their ears all day long. They're the factory workers working on the assembly line.

Toyota used to save millions of dollars a year just by giving each assembly line worker a pencil and asking her to write down ideas for improving the product or the process. If you want to hear great ideas, go spend some time with the people on the front lines of customer contact. Or, even better, go work with them for a day. You'll hear some very useful ideas in a very concentrated amount of time.

4. *From Customers* Back in the heyday of the Sony Walkman, it became fashionable for strategists and marketers to disparage the value of customer input. "If we waited for customers to tell us what they want, we'd never come up with the things they don't know they want until we make them," ran the refrain. There's

enough truth to this for it to sound convincing. The problem is, it's only half true. Customers do know what they want, they do know what they like, and if you show them new things, they'll very quickly tell you what they think. This is how Starbucks continually tests and rolls out new drinks for their coffee shops: They test them in stores that function as real-life R&D labs, and, if they work, roll them out into their "plows"—the stores that generate the real income. It's how Harrah's has transformed its gambling and entertainment business; Harrah's is the only gambling company that thinks it's in the retail business, checking regularly with shoppers to see if the offerings are to their liking. If you want to gather up great ideas—and do it at low cost—try creating listening posts where your customers can talk with you. They'll appreciate the opportunity, and you'll learn a lot.

5. From Great Companies in Other Industries The hard truth is, there aren't any new ideas. There are only new applications and smart twists on old ones. So if you want to be in the great-idea business, one way to increase your flow of ideas is to steal them. If you're in manufacturing, try visiting the best hotels in the world. Study how they "manufacture" a clean, fresh room every day. If you're in retail, check out the best-run airlines in the world. See what it takes to sell the same seat over and over again. The history of innovation is chock-full of "geniuses" who begged, borrowed, and stole ideas from one category and simply applied them to another.

Here are a few time-tested techniques for coming up with great ideas:

1. *Focus on Quantity, Not Quality* Most of us think that we need to wait for that one big, killer idea to strike. In the process, we ignore or screen out a myriad of smaller, interesting, useful, clever ideas. But the truth is, they're all worth considering. You never know when a small idea will morph into a big one. So love them all.

2. *Collect Them All* Once you get into the idea-generating business, you'll want to collect all the ideas you can get your hands on. When you think of an idea, write it down. When you see something that looks interesting, write it down. Some people carry notebooks with them. Others rely on 3×5 cards that they carry in their shirt pockets. Every once in a while, empty your notebook or your pockets into a computer file, where you can pick through what you've collected, review it, and see what really stands out.

3. *Get Outside Your Comfort Zone* If you want to find new ideas, the best thing to do is to go looking for them. Do you get ideas from magazines? Go to the nearest magazine rack, but this time buy five magazines you'd never ordinarily read. If you're an environmentalist, try reading *Guns & Ammo*. If you're a politics junkie, try reading *Scientific American*. Or, if you get your ideas from books, step outside your favorite genre. If you're a history buff, it's time for a romance novel. If you love fiction, pick up a

how-to book. Work on developing your peripheral vision. You'll be amazed at what you notice once you're in unfamiliar territory.

4. *Travel* They say that travel is broadening, but that's just the half of it. It's also *deepening*. The enemy of new ideas is the familiar. So go someplace new. If you can't actually go to an exotic country, buy the guidebook as if you were going to make the trip and read it. At a minimum, try eating at an exotic restaurant. Open up the borders of your mind.

5. *Reach Out and Touch Someone* Make a list of people you know whose minds you genuinely respect. (Over time, you'll develop more names, including people you don't know yet but whom you'd like to meet.) Make it a point to call them on a regular basis for a conversation. All you have to ask is, "What's new?" Then listen and take notes. Journalists do it all the time; it's called developing sources. It's where ideas for articles come from. Try it in your business. It works.

6. *Get Taught* Sign up for a class at a continuing-education program or a community college. Generating great ideas is part of learning, so practice learning. Just take a class. It could be in anything, from gardening to a new foreign language, from cooking to photography. You'll be in learning mode, which means your mind will be open. Once you start noticing new things in class, you'll probably notice them at work as well.

THE NEXT *DA VINCI* CODE?

Dan Brown's thriller has sold about eighteen million copies in hardcover, making it a true publishing phenomenon. And like almost all phenomena, it has created a gold rush as people try to cash in with copycats and follow-ons.

The publishing firm Little, Brown paid a previously unknown author two million dollars for a novel called *The Historian*. This is about fifty times as much as the book's author, Elizabeth Kostova, would have been paid before *The Da Vinci Code*. At the same time that Little, Brown is making a huge bet on Kostova's book, competing publishers are also lining up dozens of other books in the same vein, hoping for another hit.

The problem, as Daniel Goldin, an influential book merchandiser, sees it, is, "We think, 'What's the formula?' but of course a phenomenon always breaks the formula."

Exactly.

Sequels and knockoffs are lucky if they generate half the sales of the original. *The Rule of Four,* the first "next *Da Vinci Code,*" sold about 5 percent as well as the original.

The safest, easiest and fastest thing to do is give the market what it wants. Rushing in with the "next" whatever makes it easy for others to get buy in, and your boss will be proud of your initiative. At the same time, she'll feel relieved that you're doing something safe.

Of course, this strategy never works. If it feels safe, it certainly isn't.

DO YOU KNOW ARTHUR RUBIN?

Arthur Rubin is one of a new breed of critics. He's not employed by a newspaper or a magazine. And he doesn't review plays and musicals. Instead, Arthur reviews everything *but* plays and musicals.

He's one of a million people who are busy posting reviews online, on Amazon.com or on Epinions.com or on their own blogs. Arthur hangs out on Epinions.com, and has posted reviews of ninety-four products that have been read more than fifty thousand times.

Arthur has reviewed everything from his Maytag dishwasher to LaSalle National Bank. He has a Ph.D. in math from Caltech and there are *a million more critics out there just like him.*

How on Earth are you going to have the guts to launch anything knowing that a million critics are standing by, just itching to take your product (and you) apart?

The reviews go on your permanent record, sitting online for all to see—forever. And the most virulent reviews will spread, from prospective customer to co-worker to boss. What chance do you have to be remarkable in a world filled with nitpicky critics?

The good news is this: Criticism is now so ubiquitous that just one piece of nasty writing won't matter an awful lot. Consumers are now trained to ignore a few stray voices criticizing something new and remarkable. Yes, truly awful stuff is going to get panned and the critics will snuff you out. But for the rest of us, there's solace in knowing that most of what they write is overlooked.

More useful is this: *Ignore the critics and embrace the criticism.*

Online critics are motivated by a need for attention. They want you to notice them and to censor them and to fight back. That's the goal. So ignore the harshest ones.

But don't ignore what they say. This is valuable feedback. It's free and it's quick and it's useful. It points to a thousand ways you can dramatically improve your product—before it's too late. If you quickly embrace the essence of the feedback (without defensiveness) then you win.

Everything is a beta release. Everything you ship is version .9, just waiting for one more upgrade before it's right.

So, go ahead and ship. Then watch and read and ship again. Ignore the critics and use their criticism.

RON JOHNSON IS NOT A GENIUS . . . BUT HE HIRES THEM EVERY DAY

Five years ago, Ron Johnson did something revolutionary. He took the essence of the bars at the Ritz-Carlton hotels and put it inside of the brand-new Apple Store. The Genius Bar doesn't sell drinks. Instead, the "geniuses" (yes, they call them geniuses, and in some ways they are) at the bar provide tech support—for free.

Can you imagine how difficult this would be to sell at most organizations? "Well, we're going to hire hundreds of experts, pay them a regular salary with benefits, and have them sit behind a beautifully designed bar and dispense help and advice about Macs and iPods—free of charge."

What if Apple had charged a bit for the service, the way Best Buy does? Or what if they deliberately understaffed it, using it as a gimmick instead of a helpful service? What if they had hired the cheapest people they could find ("Hey, it's free, what do you expect?") and didn't train them very well? It's pretty easy to see that the concept would have seemed mediocre. And a failure.

Instead, Johnson's remarkable project has changed everything for Apple. More than a million people a week visit one of Apple's retail stores, and the vast majority of them don't yet own a Mac or an iPod. Instead of focusing only on barraging wary strangers with expensive advertising, Apple creates the chance for an intimate, powerful conversation. The stores are not just profitable, they are extraordinarily effective ambassadors, dramatically increasing Apple's share of the portable-music market while they shore up their computer business.

And what of the geniuses at the Genius Bar? David Isom works at one of the stores. He passed up going to law school for a stint giving free advice. One day, a shopper, apparently misunderstanding the GENIUS sign, stopped by to pitch David a plan for a solar-powered subway system. No, the geniuses don't know anything about subways. But Ron Johnson understands that extremism in the name of retail success is genius indeed.

TWO KINDS OF ORGANIZATIONS

Have you ever seen a recumbent bicycle? They look sort of like *Easy Rider*-style chopper motorcycles, but the seat is even more reclined and there's no engine, except the driver.

It turns out that recumbent bikes are faster, more comfortable, and more fun to ride than the bikes we all grew up with. Speed aside, for anyone with back trouble, neck trouble, or the need to make a spectacle of himself, a recumbent bicycle is a great choice. There are more than a dozen "major" manufacturers of the bikes, each producing a few hundred or a few thousand recumbents a year. In total, the industry accounts for less than 1 percent of all bikes sold.

Here's the surprising problem: Recumbent bikes are taking off. At InterWest 2005, the giant bike show held every year in Las Vegas, all the major traditional-bike manufacturers were showing off bikes that are beginning to look more and more like recumbents. They're just responding to the changing market. Aging baby boomers don't want a Lance Armstrong bike—instead, they want to be comfortable. So brands like Trek and Giant (which sell, in one day, as many bikes as most recumbent companies do in a year) are starting to push their designs in the recumbent direction.

So why is this a problem? Why isn't this great news for the existing recumbent manufacturers? After all, they're already good at building the bikes people want.

It's a problem because the long-suffering existing manufacturers are delighted that the marketplace has finally seen the light. "We were right!" they're thinking, and they're responding to the competitive pressure of traditional-bike manufacturers' going after recumbents by making *their* recumbent bikes more like traditional ones. In essence, they're emulating Trek while Trek is emulating them.

They're going to get crushed.

There are two kinds of organizations. One kind likes to be on the cutting edge, to do what hasn't been done before, to embrace the new. The other kind fears that, and holds back to allow someone else to go first.

The United Way is facing tough times because they're afraid to change. The Saddleback Church in California is doing wonderfully (10,000 percent growth over the last few years) because they love to change.

The recumbent-bicycle companies aren't organized to compete on price and distribution and consistency. They should let the Treks and the Giants of the world teach everyone what to buy, while they keep making the expensive, quirky stuff for the real afi-cionados. As the market gets bigger, they'll thrive. They're good at staying on the edge, and they should stay there.

Companies that are good at being edgy will always find a way to thrive. The sure way to fail, it seems, is to attempt to compro-mise that affinity for edginess for the mass market. It's harder than it looks.

But what if your organization embraces its stuckness? What's it going to take for you to start changing? What do you do when the market is moving *away* from you, not toward you? It seems to me that if you wait too long, it'll be too late to do much of any-thing at all. Instead, recognize that change is coming, that the re-ality you operate in is dying out, and start practicing how to do the next big thing.

Betting on change is always the safest bet available.

GET STARTED FAST AND CHEAP

The ubiquitous, pocket-width, burgundy-colored restaurant guide the Zagat Survey—called by *The New York Times* "a necessity second only to a valid credit card"—seems like the kind of big idea that started with a substantial financial investment, a major marketing move, and the unbridled support of restaurant industry folks. It didn't, though.

Creators Tim and Nina Zagat started collecting insight from their foodie friends in 1979 and, a few years later, began selling the collective advice in the form of the first New York City Zagat Survey from their station wagon. (Not every company has its roots in the garage!)

The Zagats, both practicing corporate lawyers, had no agent, no publisher, and no money to spend on advertising. Relying on a unique idea (rating a restaurant on the basis of thousands of experiences, not one reviewer), word-of-mouth marketing, and some good free publicity (after a 1985 cover story in *New York* magazine sales jumped from 40,000 a year to more than 75,000 a month), the Zagats grew their enterprise from a New York–based food guide with a cult following into the world's best-selling publisher of restaurant guides.

Zagat now offers guides to dining in cities from San Francisco to Shanghai and has expanded to survey hotels, airlines, golf courses, and more. The guide is now available on the Web and voting has moved online, attracting more than 250,000 voters worldwide. And even now, with proven success and deeper pockets, Zagat continues to use fast, inexpensive, and scalable ways to help it grow, such as not investing in pricey back-end systems, but using newer, cheaper, and simpler Web-based services instead.

Fast and cheap doesn't mean chintzy or short-term. It just means you make your mistakes quickly and inexpensively and get them over with.

STEVEN SAVAGE IS NOT MORE CREATIVE THAN YOU ARE

Have you persuaded yourself that you're not creative? That you have to leave creativity to the experts?

Somewhere along the way, a boss or a parent or a friend persuaded you that you are boring. That you can't plan an original dinner party, name an original product, design an original car, or even write an original paragraph.

This, of course, is utter nonsense. All four-year-olds are creative. But over time, the system burns it out of them. The system trains us to keep our mouths shut or we'll get picked on, called on, or laughed at. So we learn to bury that creativity.

On to Steven Savage. Savage runs a Web site (www.seventh sanctum.com) that makes it easy for people designing cartoons and multiplayer games to dream up names, settings, and situations. For example, here are ten evil characters the system created: Auazgon, Elrthall, Hanithmaet, Megorn, Namoru, Nglangond, Shaurturo, Thethunauli, Thia, Thulangorirorn. According to his planet generator, they are from the planet Sextus Tosola Upsilon.

Obviously, the computer-naming programs he's running are simple and stupid. All they do is take proven ideas and rub them up against each other.

Exactly.

Organizations don't get stuck because their employees aren't creative. Creativity is mostly persistent iteration and juxtaposition. What messes things up is our self-censorship and organizations' innate tendency to put the brakes on something that's remarkable.

The next time you want to criticize yourself for being dull, stop. Criticize yourself (and your organization) for being scared instead.

THE PROBLEM WITH COMPROMISE

Any organization with more than one person in it is a place of compromise. If you want to get something done, a project okayed, a budget approved, a product sold, you're going to have to compromise.

Most of the time, it seems as though half is better than none. If you refuse to compromise, nothing happens. And this desire to make it happen explains why so many things are mediocre. It tells us why it's so hard to make something remarkable, and why the remarkable succeeds so easily. Because everything is a compromise, everything is sort of mediocre, isn't it?

The wireless Internet access at the Denver airport has compromise written all over it. I'm sure that when it was first designed (probably by a lone engineer in a cubicle), it was simple and fast and easy to use. Today, however, it takes at least a dozen clicks to get started. You need to enter a user name and ID not once, but twice. And your ID must be at least eight characters long and include numbers *and* a special character like $, %, or #. So, some-

thing like "$3eVh!" is not secure enough becaus
Huh? This isn't your credit rating you're protec
the right to spend nine dollars and go online.

At every step along the way, each compromise to the sign-on
system seemed reasonable. At each step, the evolution of the design was simple: Either the project manager had to go along with
the needs of this or that person (and the boss) or risk having the
project canceled. What would you do? All those compromises
may have made each person happy, but the final product was
something that absolutely no one liked.

The first step to fighting back is understanding how compromise corrupts the things you're so busy building. More often than
not, half is actually worse than none. More often than not, you're
better off doing nothing than shipping something that is just average. The project manager in Denver should have just stopped
the project and let the chorus of complaints from passengers sink
in to make the case for doing things the right way from the start.

Twenty years ago, Japanese car companies solved their quality
control problem using a technique called Kanban. Instead of following the American technique of having plenty of spare parts on
the assembly line (workers were told to just discard a screw if it
didn't fit right), the Japanese adopted a fundamentally different
strategy. They kept only *one* necessary part at a time on the assembly line. If the part wasn't perfect, the entire assembly line
stopped until a new part arrived.

The Americans said that this was insane. Everyone knew that
keeping the assembly line moving was the only way to make a car

efficiently. If a finished car wasn't good enough, then you fixed it after it was assembled.

What Toyota and Honda understood was that the act of stopping the assembly line would send a powerful signal to every worker and to every supplier. Sure enough, the line didn't have to stop very often. Every part improved in quality, because no one wanted to be responsible for shutting the operation down. As a result, better parts improved every car as well. With Kanban, very few cars left the assembly line in need of later reworking. It turned out to be cheaper and faster to build cars right the first time than it was to fix them later.

You might try the same thing in your organization. Refuse to compromise. See what happens. For a while, the assembly line will slow down or even stop. Things won't ship, products will get stuck in development. And then a funny thing will happen: People will begin to understand that compromising the products just to keep the system working is stupid. The only reason the system exists is so that you can make the things you make, right? So *if the system is demeaning your work, change the system.*

THE POWER OF DUMB IDEAS

This will be the dumbest riff on marketing you will ever read. If you're lucky.

Marketing is overwhelmed by complexity, and marketers' predisposition toward creativity only complicates their job, their companies' operations, and their own lives even more.

Ten years ago, the challenges were *merely*:

- the advance of the five-hundred-channel universe
- reconciling the historic tensions between marketing and sales
- calculating the return on advertising investment
- keeping abreast of fickle public taste

Today, a quick look at Google indicates that we're grappling with an eight-billion-channel world. The distinction between marketing and sales has evaporated in the face of direct-marketing technologies that brand products, take orders, and fulfill them at the same time.

Even worse, there is no more public taste. There are only publics' tastes, which are ever more atomized, specific, and hard to fathom.

David Ogilvy's contention that "it takes a big idea to attract the attention of consumers and get them to buy your product" no longer applies. His fellow advertising guru Bill Bernbach's belief that, in marketing, "not to be different is virtually suicidal" today itself may be suicidal in and of itself.

The solution to marketing's current ills is not more creativity. It's less.

Novelty for the sake of novelty is not only risky, it's more often than not a recipe for irrelevance. A study of 1,300 publicly traded U.S. companies in fifty-five industries by Chuck Lucier, senior vice president emeritus at Booz Allen Hamilton, found that only four broad ideas, copied over and over again in one sector after another, accounted for 80 percent of the breakout businesses created between 1965 and 1995: power retailing, megabranding, focus/simplify/standardize, and the value chain bypass. True, the big-box store may not be the most original concept on Earth—which is exactly the point! Originality hasn't mattered a whit to the customers, employees, and shareholders who have enjoyed its application in consumer electronics (Circuit City), home improvement (Home Depot), and office supplies (Staples).

So what is the simple, dumb truth?

Imitation Across Industries Is More Efficient and Effective Than Blue-Sky Creativity and Innovation If you accept that one million monkeys pounding on keyboards for one thousand years will eventually, accidentally produce a ton of gibberish and one Shakespearean sonnet, you must also accept the converse: that a lone creative individual racking her brain will produce much less gibberish, and nothing profound. Appropriating existing marketing concepts is cheaper—and certainly quicker to implement—than developing new ones. The secret is bringing a great idea from another market or industry to your market or your industry.

The Energy Isn't in the Idea; it's in the Execution Every manager, from the middle on up, knows that the secret to success lies not in strategy, but in galvanizing a team to implement the strategy. Lucier's research on breakout businesses also showed that the winning companies in each market were those that put together a winning business system around the unoriginal ideas. The hard work of marketing lies not in developing a groundbreaking product or the communications scheme for it, but in coordinating the efforts of R&D, manufacturing, finance, communications, sales, or some set of subunits. Do this once, and you've created a cross-functional team that knows how to do it over and over again, and whose enthusiasm itself communicates volumes.

You Must Create True Believers Before You Can Win New Converts I once asked the president of a major U.S. auto company whether any studies had been done to determine which factors distinguished superior salespeople from average salespeople. He responded that the only research he'd ever seen found no differences in age, education, sex, race, or family background, but did reveal one distinct variable: the number of times the individual went back and attempted to close the sale. Faith in yourself and in your colleagues is a necessary predisposition for marketers; the best ones convey that faith outward, eventually subsuming their customers and clients. The most powerful marketing ideas create and reinforce that kind of faith.

It's Your Context That Counts The big idea doesn't have to be the brand-new idea. Something common to the world at large may be very new to you and your organization. This is more than enough to galvanize the team, create faith, and build the world's greatest marketing department.

Three Dumb Ideas:
This may be a dumb idea, but what if we take our company's private annual review and turn it into a full-blown, beautifully designed, public annual report? Surely, it would communicate our changes and strengths to the outside world—and it would also create immense new pride inside our globally dispersed company, more understanding of our strategy, and greater consistency in our numerous marketing efforts.

This may be a dumb idea, but what if we publish a book of our research and writing on enterprise resilience—not with a mainstream publisher who'll take a year to get from manuscript to finished product, but by ourselves? Using existing vendors in graphic design, print-on-demand production, and online sales, we could complete the book in six weeks, stirring the members on the team to personally take it to their clients, discuss its contents, and build their business. In two years, we could publish six books, create our own imprint, sell thousands of copies, distribute tens of thousands more, garner major-media reviews, and create a publishing capability in a nonpublishing company.

This may be a dumb idea, but what if we create a diagnostic tool that uses principles of organizational economics to measure the effectiveness of large companies, then put it on the Web so that individuals can assess their own firms' abilities? Less than a year later, there could be a 60,000-profile database, segmentable by country, sector, and function—and a thriving global practice in "Org DNA."

An annual report. A book. An online survey. We did it well, and we did it together, knitting our internal communities and our external markets into a quilt that may be patchwork, but is exquisitely patterned nonetheless. This is the simplicity on the other side of marketing's complexity.

Dumb enough for you?

INSIDE OUT/OUTSIDE IN

John Seely Brown is the former head of Xerox PARC and a renowned thinker and writer on the art of management. He is deservedly famous for a number of statements. The one I like best is, "The job of the leader isn't just to make decisions, it's to make sense."

Making sense is actually everyone's job. The better you are at it, the better you'll do in the working world.

Can you connect the invisible dots? Can you improve the signal-to-noise ratio in all the data that's streaming at you? Take all the information that comes at you in the course of just one day. The morning newspaper: How many do you read? Two? Three? There's the *Times* and the *Journal*, plus your hometown paper. What about magazines? *Fortune, Forbes, BusinessWeek, Fast Company*? How about professional journals and industry-specific publications like *Variety, Advertising Age, Adweek, Institutional Investor, CEO, CFO, CIO*? Do you try to keep up with weekly newsmagazines like *Time, Newsweek, U.S. News & World Report, The Economist*? What do you read for fun? Magazines about golf, fishing or hunting, home decoration or design, health and fitness, or just gossip? Do you watch TV? The nightly news? Sports or made-for-TV movies? How about e-mail? Get a few of those each day, do you?

Now, from all that stuff, how good are you at making sense?

Can you see the patterns and themes as they emerge? Can you connect the front page of the *Times* with the e-mail coming over the Net to your latest sales figures to new sociological trends and make a prediction about what you, your team, your company need to do next?

Because that's the art of making sense in the lives of most businesspeople, whether they see it like that or not.

Or at least it has been.

The premise is that your job as a leader, a sensor, a future finder, is to weave these outside threads together faster, smarter, and better than the competition. That's the way it has been—at least up until now. Smart businesspeople making sense of the world, gathering and synthesizing external data.

Now we get to the interesting part.

Think of it as quantum mechanics come to business sense making.

Now the sense maker is *part* of the sense making.

Now the interior landscape is part of the connect-the-dots effort.

In other words, now the job of the business leader isn't just to gaze *out* at a dizzying world full of streaming data. It's to gaze *in*, at the long-ignored interior landscape.

Hello in there! What's going on?

What are all the creative urges that have burrowed way down deep? The desire to draw or paint, write a film script or master photography? Not enough hours in the day to learn how to play guitar or study Japanese?

Did you always want to look into the history of the opera? Or try to figure out some of the other things your PC can do besides process words? Or are you like one of the founders of Google, who always wanted to go to circus school—and finally did?

The way the world works now, the way the rules of engagement operate, you can't claim to make sense out of the exterior without booking voyages into the interior. Think about it: How can you understand "it" if you haven't made any effort to understand "you"? Because what you're really doing is establishing a living, electrical, vital, energetic connection between it and you. You're creating both of them, simultaneously. A lot like quantum physics.

So what to do?

Do what Jim Collins did when he was a student. Treat yourself like an experiment, like your very own lab rat. Do you dream at night? Start writing them down.

Do you wish you could be a writer? You are! Reserve an hour every day to record your thoughts in a special file on your PC. Build up a journal, an inventory of your inner life.

When was the last time you read a novel—a real novel, not one of those paperback-thriller pieces of crap? Pick up some serious fiction and let it work its emotional magic on your overly rational mind.

How many museums or art galleries have you visited in the last six months? How many contemporary artists can you name? If you only know the names of your competitors, and you can't name a single artist, your outer and inner life are seriously out of balance.

Take time to go inside. Learn to meditate, to do yoga. Take time to exercise—you think you're toning your body, but you're also redirecting your mind. Gradually, over time, you'll find that you can make more and better sense of what's outside and what's inside. And what's the difference.

THE STUDENT BECOMES
THE TEACHER

I'm in Seattle. It's January, and a light rain is falling. Dampness pervades everything that I see and sense.

I'm a young engineer traveling with my company's chief technical officer. This is day three of a stressful four-day business trip. Our work is done, but I find myself standing with Jim in the midst of a primordial giant-redwood forest somewhere near Mount Rainier. We are about a mile from the nearest road and the trees reach up as high as anyone can see. Moss and vegetation consume those giants that have succumbed to the environment.

How did I get here and what was I doing?

I am listening to dead silence. This is a life-changing time that I will be forever grateful for—a master and his student experiencing the world in the most unconventional way. Jim is a visionary, a remarkable leader—a teacher, a scientist, a philosopher, an executive, and a prolific innovator. We spend two hours in the for-

est, the first thirty minutes standing in silence, becomir
with the environment. Over the next ninety minutes, Jim shares
his philosophies on leadership. His message is simple but elo-
quent:

- Be impatient, don't tolerate mediocrity.
- Be confident in your ability—you can make a difference in
  the world.
- Have extreme passion for your work and those you are work-
  ing with.
- Never compromise your integrity.
- Risk is the only reward—without risk, there is no benefit.
- Expect isolation, separation, and intolerance.
- Take the time to know and connect with worlds that are vastly
  different from yours—your greatest discoveries reside there.
- Dare to be different.

Within twelve months of those moments of discovery in Seattle, the master resigned his position at the peak of his career due
to ethical and philosophical differences. A man of principle, Jim
would never compromise his integrity at any cost.

Twenty years later, the student has become the master. I
find myself scaling the last set of steps to the top of the Eiffel
Tower, sharing the wisdom acquired twenty years prior in that
deep, dark Northwest forest with a truly remarkable student
preparing to lead the next generation. The messages still apply

today, even though we exist in a vastly different world. Jim's wisdom was timeless and it is my responsibility to keep the message alive.

Thank you, Jim, wherever you are. I am proud to have known you.

FIRE THE GATEKEEPERS

As John Perry Barlow or John Patrick once told me (I forget which), the World Wide Web isn't about pages, it's about people. It isn't about information, it's about the ideas and insights of people around the world.

Regardless of whether you regularly read Salon.com, *The New York Times* online, or any number of frequently updated blogs and personal Web sites, the true value of your experience, evolution, and insight doesn't lie in the words you read on the screen but in the minds of the people who write them, as well as your reaction to their writing. We as readers need and deserve to know who those people are. And we need to recognize, reach out to, and embrace them.

In the blog world, on the Web, such outreach is easy. We can see who writes what, and many of the better blogs are tightly tied to the beliefs, knowledge, and lives of their proprietors and contributors. Feedback loops are short. Online newspapers and magazines are much the same. For the most part, we can easily and effortlessly make contact, correspond, and collaborate with people like Dan Gillmor (formerly with the *San Jose Mercury News*), Eric Zorn (*Chicago Tribune*), and others with just a few simple keystrokes.

But with most media — including Web sites, newspapers, magazines, books, music, and film — gatekeepers stand between us and the meaning makers. We need to fire the gatekeepers.

Entire industries and professions exist to keep us from interacting with the people we need to know: politicians, business leaders, writers, musicians, and other cultural creatives — people who make things happen and contribute to (and reflect) our collective reality. Traditional media, even, is largely designed to keep us from the knowledge we need, not to facilitate learning. So we must find a way around the approved channels of communication — the PR agencies, media trainers, publishing houses, record labels, film producers, and so on.

This is already happening online as some media and meaning makers reach out to us. But if they're not reaching out — if it's not in the vested interest of the organizations controlling the more economically lucrative modes of promotion and distribution — we need to help these thinkers and doers to do so anyway. We need to reach out to them.

In California, Hyland Baron, an independent arts, economic, and urban-development-oriented community organizer, reads the *Oakland Tribune* religiously. She underlines people's names, details about projects, and other useful information. Then she writes those people e-mails or letters or calls them on the phone with recommended resources, incentives for introductions, and other expressions of support and congratulations.

I do the same thing. If I read a book I've found personally or professionally important and useful, I try to track down the author. If a piece of music affects me, I reach out to thank the artist for their effort. And if I want to meet, learn more from, or help someone I encounter online or off-line, I write to them.

I do this not as a fan but as a comrade, as a coconspirator. Because if someone else's work has improved *my* life or *my* work, it is my responsibility as a consumer, customer, and fellow creator to help improve their lives and work in kind. By doing so, I don't just benefit them, I benefit myself. Perhaps an idea, introduction, or resource will inspire and lead them to create additional media that you—and others—can tap into and use. You never know.

Such an approach to life requires an assumption of indirect reciprocity. We must assume that the people who make things happen are visible, accessible, and responsible to those who use their tools to make still more things happen. It also suggests that we need to open ourselves to such outreach from those who wish to approach us.

Once we fire the gatekeepers, we can keep the gates of inspiration, implementation, and interaction open.

STOP BEING ORDINARY

The first step to becoming extraordinary of course is simply to *stop being ordinary*. You'd certainly like to have remarkable returns as an organization, wouldn't you? And extraordinary rewards as an individual, right? Then start behaving remarkably.

So, where to begin? Here are five quick suggestions:

1. *Avidly Collect Firsthand Experiences* Be your own Sherlock Holmes. Take pains to observe and understand nuances from the front lines of your business. Even in a room full of industry experts, you're still the master of your own personal experiences. Don't be shy about adding your own insights to the mix. Too busy to spend time in the field? Think again. A. G. Lafley, CEO of $50 billion Procter & Gamble, still regularly finds time to visit individual homes and talk with customers to keep current on what really matters to people. He could obviously delegate that role,

but he finds the time to make his own firsthand observations because he knows they're important. So can you.

2. *Practice the Zen Principle of "Beginner's Mind"* People with a thirst for learning can momentarily set aside what they "know." They often have extensive academic backgrounds and ample professional experience, but they manage to look past tradition and preconceived notions. They're confident in their knowledge, yet willing to challenge it when confronted with new information.

3. *Keep an "Idea Wallet" So You Don't Lose Momentary Insights* Real-world anthropologists carry a field notebook and a camera to record their discoveries. Try recording ideas in real time—on your PDA, or even on a folded sheet of paper you keep in your back pocket.

4. *Be a Proactive "Idea Broker" and Practice Continuous Cross-Pollination* Think in metaphors to apply the lessons you learn from one context to another. Try to give equal weight to learning and collaborating so that you can be a conduit for fresh ideas.

5. *Embrace the Power of Storytelling to Bring It All Together* Storytelling has an emotional appeal that trumps all the raw data in the world. Medtronic, a blue-chip medical-technology company, reports that when their teams need an extra spark, they bring in patients and ask them to talk about how a Medtronic

product changed their lives. The results are positively electric. These life-affirming stories leave hardly a dry eye in the house, and the entire Medtronic team returns to work with renewed energy, motivated to do their absolute best.

So, make a New Year's resolution that matters, and stick with it: Reject routine and set your team on its own remarkable course, one grounded in human inspiration, storytelling, and radical collaboration that will lead you to distinction.

THE REMARKABILITY
OF MEMORIES

In 2004, the band Phish ended its twenty-one-year music career by playing two concerts on the mud-soaked hills of Vermont. Due to days of rain, which made for flooded fields and standstill traffic, thousands of fans abandoned their cars on the highway and walked for miles to hear the last sounds of their favorite band. During the final set, the band's keyboardist, Page McConnell, actually broke down crying as he tried to get through a song. The band took their bows after the encore and officially said good-bye to Phish, promising to reinvent themselves in other genres, formats, and acts.

That October, the band Deep Purple played a series of dates in Russia, with fifty-nine-year old lead singer Ian Gillian—a bandanna covering his now receding hairline—still attempting to "rock." Formed in 1968 in Germany, this British group had worldwide hits like "In Rock," "Black Night," "Fireball," and "Machine Head." With a newfound popularity in previously off-limit markets, the band was reliving the days of its youth—and shattering thousands of middle-aged suburbanites' images of them, perceptions based on what Deep Purple was like in the seventies.

In 1998, the cast of *Seinfeld* decided that it was time to end their amazing run. The show was the cornerstone of Thursday night television for millions of Americans, and was still at the top of the Nielsen ratings, but the cast publicly stated that they wanted to end on a high note, without creating new shows that lacked comedic genius. They were afraid of getting tired. *Seinfeld* has now generated more than a billion dollars through syndication and DVD sales.

At the same time that *Seinfeld* and Phish decide to go out on top, brands like Barbie struggle to meet expectations. For Barbie, at least, all of Mattel's product extensions and brand saturation aren't making memories that lead to purchases. Sales are down $14 million in just a year. Maybe Mattel should accept what consumers are telling them: "Slow down, we need a break." Maybe they should stop altogether.

The point here is that your blockbuster of yesterday could very well be getting in the way of tomorrow's blockbuster. The cash cow makes it easy to resist the temptation (and risk) of trying something new.

Sometimes being remarkable is about knowing when it's time to move on and force your team to invent the next great thing instead of milking yesterday's hit just a little too long.

THE POWER OF SMALL STEPS

Being remarkable is difficult because you often must take small steps rather than rely on huge leaps. Small steps are not for the impatient, though.

Try to imagine a group of twenty women in Rwanda. They were single mothers, all of them poor, all of them living at the bottom of the socioeconomic ladder. Some people called them prostitutes as a way of dismissing them, making them even more invisible in a society filled with invisible women. These twenty women, though, were trying to get out from under. They had all joined a program that was focused on empowering single mothers.

These twenty women were working as employees for an organization trying to find single mothers some kind of "income-generating opportunity" (the catchphrase in Africa for anything people can think of to increase women's income). Problem was, most of the UN development workers didn't know how to run a business and, if they were really honest with themselves, many of them had little faith that these twenty women (and others like them) could do anything productive. These women were stuck, dependent on the old charity model, which, despite the best of intentions, kept them in poverty.

The group wore distinctive green gingham smock dresses and met each day in a uniquely depressing little house in a popular quarter of Kigali. The area was called Nyamirambo and it consisted of a main street with small homes painted in Candy Land colors, most of them serving as businesses too—tailors, shoemakers, radio repair shops, and not much else. From this main, paved road, lots of dirt roads wound back into the hills, where most of the people in the capital city of Kigali actually lived.

Each morning, the women would make their goods (in essence, they took dough and made it into different shapes and fried it.) They made doughnuts, just doughnuts, but in lots of different shapes.

As luck would have it, the women's group was run by a dynamo named Prisca. Prisca abhorred the dependence on charity and handouts that kept her group stuck, but didn't know how to change the model. She was a good bookkeeper, meticulously recording all of the costs incurred and income earned by the bakery and tallying weekly results. Two things were striking. Each woman earned the same amount—fifty cents a day—regardless of how many doughnuts she sold. At the same time, weekly losses had been increasing consistently for at least a year. On average, the bakery grossed about $100 a day among the twenty saleswomen. Monthly losses averaged about $625.

How did the bakery survive? Another part of the women's

group sewed and rented bridal gowns and this helped cover some of the losses, but mostly they depended on support from the local Catholic charity. Prisca knew that this couldn't last forever: Sooner or later, the nuns would get tired of keeping the support going just to employ two dozen people at half the minimum wage.

Prisca decided that good intentions weren't helping anyone. Her goal became the same as that of any business: Increase sales and cut costs. To increase sales we (yes, "we." I was there. And this is my story too) persuade Consolata, a tall, elegant woman of few words, to increase her sales effort. She visits at least five embassies and most of the UN agencies. Unicef promised to order baked goods every day. Though their office was not in the center of town, Consolata promised to send a woman with goods each day at midmorning.

On the first day of embracing the new mind-set, the group nearly doubled the places to which the women generally go to solicit business. We're on our way.

The next morning at the bakery, the women work behind the little house, squatting on their heels, cooking in a traditional wok-like pot over an open fire. They gossip to one another, creating a lovely melody to accompany the hot oil crackling as the lumps of dough are put into the pan. By eight o'clock, other members of the group arrive to clean, help with cooking, and organize the freshly made goods into individual buckets. Each woman is responsible for taking what she can sell and then returning the leftovers, though no system exists to track inventory. By nine or so, most of the twenty women have taken a crowded minibus into town, holding bright orange buckets and big thermoses of tea on their laps.

We talk about marketing and pitching sales and finding new places to expand markets and reach more customers. I suggest that we turn the house that we use into a standing bakery where people in Nyamirambo can stop by and purchase a *sambusa* and have a cup of tea. They like the idea but don't know how we'll do it.

We try to role-play. Gaudence, always so gloomy, wants to be the person who remains at the bakery, so she is first to volunteer. We talk about eye contact, inviting the customer to see the products, letting him know the prices. Gaudence looks uncomfortable and the other women laugh.

"Okay," I say, "let's put someone else on the spot. Consolata, I'm sitting next to you on the minibus, feeling hungry. Can you sell me something before I get off the bus?"

The room roars with laughter at the thought. "No," she says, "that is too difficult."

"Why?" I ask.

"Because women do not just ask strangers to buy things on buses."

"Why not?"

They cannot stop laughing now. "Because that is not polite."

I drop it. For now.

We return to our class on who the customer is, how to market, and how to look at a customer and convince her to buy something. The more animated I become, the harder the women laugh. "Okay," I ask, "what is going on?"

Prisca, always ready to be frank, answers. "You are so American. Here, women won't look someone in the eye, won't talk to someone they don't know. It is like that here, you have to accept it."

"Okay, let me show you," I say. I take a bucket into the street outside and start talking to people as they pass me. In no time, I sell ten doughnuts, more than some of the women sold all day. "Look," I say, "it is easy if you market."

I can feel Prisca looking at me as the women talk among themselves. She laughs, telling me that the women think that no one will say no to an American selling them things on the streets of Nyamirambo. There is too much novelty in that. But no one even wants to look at a poor woman selling snacks out of a bucket.

The attributes of entrepreneurship—risk taking, innovation, vision—are both cultural and learned. Rwanda's culture leaves little room for individualism or innovation. This is not a trading society, not a place that values rapid change. The women at the bakery simply desire to bring their goods to the offices and collect their meager pay to bring home to their families.

I refuse to accept this. We run competitions for the women to see who can sell the most, but no one will participate. We hold training sessions on how to treat customers, but the response is tepid, at best. We give pep talks every Friday and explain our vision, just in case someone forgot it, but no one can understand my French.

We then introduce a more transparent accounting system. We make pay completely contingent on what is sold and how costs are controlled, so that the success of this venture really does become the responsibility of the women who, in essence, own the bakery.

In the following weeks, we start making real progress. I have gained respect from the women with this new toughness and clarity. We all know the rules now and finally, the plan seems to be working. Sales skyrocket and we gain new customers weekly. At the same time, we know that in a small city like Kigali, our base of customers is fairly limited. So we decide to do two things. First, we will finally make the little building itself a real bakery where people from the neighborhood can come to buy. Then we make a commitment to expand and sell other goods that people might want to eat. In the end, it is all the same—cash in, cash out, knowing the market, expanding where you can, and delivering quality.

Despite some bumps, within six months we have cornered the snack market in Kigali, expanding from our repertoire of fried dough in a variety of shapes to making cassava chips, banana chips, and peanut butter. We buy plastic containers from the local honey factory for the peanut butter and people came from all over to buy it. We even venture into sorghum bread and hit it big with the Europeans in town. The women are now earning four times the daily minimum wage and there is no stopping us.

And every one of those women became remarkable within her own right. They could choose to say no, they could choose to say yes, they could make their own decisions. They could believe in who they were and have a much greater say in who they wanted to be. Which, at the end of the day, is what we all want, rich or poor, from the United States or from a little corner of Rwanda.

THE FEARLESS FLIGHT
OF LITTLE MAX

In the early 1980s, the Soviet Union began letting some of its citizens emigrate to the United States. A surprisingly large number of those that came over were talented engineers, draftspeople and factory production workers. One company in Buffalo, New York, hired a number of the Russian immigrants to work in their factory.

To make their transition to America a little easier, the company's CEO and his wife would invite the Russian employees' families over to their house to celebrate various holidays during the year. Gregory (a new employee) came with his family, including little Max, his ebullient three-year-old son. There were about twenty people there for dinner. The adults congregated in the living room while the kids played tag in the kitchen, running circles around the kitchen table, which was piled high with food and drink.

The table had no chairs—they were all in the living room.

The kids didn't care. They were having fun chasing Max. He was frustrated because his size made him an easy target.

Max came up with a plan. First, as fast as his little feet would carry him, he headed to the living room. The other kids gave pursuit, tearing their way through the crowd. They were gaining on him. Max didn't hesitate. He turned and headed back to the kitchen. The parents watched, aghast, as Max headed directly for the kitchen table. He wasn't slowing down.

Max didn't miss a step. He ran at full speed right under the table, the tabletop missing his head by less than an inch. It was a triumph that the other kids would never forget. It was like an action movie, where the hero's car just fits into the tunnel while the evildoers crash into the overpass.

The question I've asked myself a million times is this: "How did Max know he'd fit?" What if he had hit the table? It goes against all our instincts to pull a stunt like that—because we're grown-ups.

The answer, it turns out, is simple. Max *didn't* know. All he knew was that if he was going to pull this stunt off, he'd have to do it at full speed. Feeling it out, going slow just to be sure it would be okay, was a compromise that would make the entire effort worthless.

Max's lesson wasn't wasted on his audience. Years later, when the company was faced with the opportunity to buy a computer-controlled laser cutter, they had three choices. The obvious, safe choice was to let the competition go first and see what would happen, then follow along if it worked. The second, compromised choice was to buy the cheap, mediocre cutter and see if it made sense to eventually buy the right machine. Third, the company could invest 25 percent of its equity and buy the cutter that would do the job.

What would Max do? They bought the big cutter. It saved the company.

Sometimes, compromise is worse than doing nothing, and leaping into the unknown with all the enthusiasm and naiveté of a toddler is the best thing you can do.

SOME THINGS JUST DON'T TRANSLATE!

My friend Giorgio has a housewares business. He's Italian, and he started near his home in a small town in Italy. The business has grown quite consistently over the past twenty years or so. He's expanded well beyond where he started to other cities in Italy, always delighting his customers and turning a good profit.

His passion is for functional items that are beautifully handcrafted, that elusive combination of good looks and nice "feel" in the hand. As he's continued to pursue this, the company has taken on a distinct sensibility and style. My guests always comment when they eat with one of Giorgio's forks or drink from one of his espresso cups—the products consistently echo the brand.

American tourists shopped in Giorgio's stores in various parts of Italy and, not surprisingly, soon they became an overwhelming voice, suggesting, asking, and sometimes begging for him to expand to the United States. For years he resisted. Business was good in Italy and, of course, the lifestyle was fairly simple, so it was easy enough for him to keep expanding on home turf. But when the chorus became too loud to ignore, he opened his first stateside store, just outside of Washington D.C.

The sense of excitement and curiosity was far beyond anything he ever imagined. Sometimes people would wait in line for hours before the store opened! But sales were well below what he'd anticipated based on the foot traffic he was getting.

Baffled, he spent days in the store talking to prospective customers, and watching them. They wandered the aisles gazing, smiling, touching most of the merchandise—and buying very little. Days went by and he didn't know how to interpret what was happening. He told me, "I started to wonder, Did people think this was a museum and not a store?" So he decided to dig in deeper and spend time in one area. He focused on glassware.

Giorgio positioned himself so that he had a perfect view of the four aisles and three stands where the glasses were displayed. Over and over again he watched people pick up a package of six-ounce drinking glasses that came six to a package, and put them back. Then they would go to the sixteen-ounce vases, which were sold individually. The customers, looking puzzled, would pick them up and put them back, too. Typically, they would go back and forth between these two items, talk amongst themselves, and ultimately walk away, buying neither.

When he couldn't bear it any longer, Giorgio introduced himself to one of them and asked, "How are you finding the store? The merchandise? The glasses and the vases?" The customer said, "They're beautiful, but I don't understand why you're selling the bud vases as a package of six!" Surprised, Giorgio said, "What did you say?" The customer repeated, this time with a bit more enthusiasm, "You're selling these adorable bud vases as a package of six. Maybe I could use two or three, but I don't really know how I would ever use six!" She continued, "The water glasses are also very nice and I really like them, but I would expect to find these in a package of four or six. No one expects to buy everyday water glasses one at a time. It's not very practical!"

In that instant my Italian friend understood that he had truly arrived in America. What this prospective customer saw as a bud vase was a drinking glass for Giorgio and for people all over Italy, so of course it was sold in a package of six. And what were in Italy easily understood as flower vases were water glasses to Americans with larger, thirstier tastes. Perfecto! This explained so much. Certainly no one would buy a six-pack of bud vases.

Giorgio summarized it all when he said, "The product is what the customer thinks it is, and what *I* think has little to do with that. I can only learn from the customer what they expect." Studying and listening to people's reactions to the product, to how it's packaged and how it's priced, can make the difference between a thriving business and a warehouse of inert inventory. A product isn't for everyone, it's for someone.

BORING

The enemy of the big moo is *boring*. To the marketer, boring means safe and predictable, highly focused, and with little downside risk. Of course, the opposite is true.

When Apple launched the iPod Shuffle, they were selling fun. It certainly wasn't a product that anyone truly needed. The iPod Shuffle is a little luxury, a fashion item in off-white that's supposed to be fun to use, fun to buy, and fun to think about. It's around the size of a stack of four pieces of Juicy Fruit gum and comes in a neat little box.

Having been burned in the past on marketing claims about disk size and battery life, Apple's lawyers had the marketers list a bunch of disclaimers on the Apple Web site. Stuff like, "Music capacity is based on 4 minutes per song and 128Kbps AAC encoding." But right in the middle of the disclaimers, in tiny little gray type, it said, "Do not eat iPod Shuffle."

This is funny. It's fun. It's the sort of inside joke that one Apple fanatic might point out to another. In fact, people started blogging about it. The joke was a subtle reminder of the tiny size of the Shuffle, but it also showed a subtle disdain for the lawyers.

Guess what? A few weeks later, the disclaimer was gone.

Boring.

The best way to find your big moo is to lighten up. A lot. Start small, but start. Don't take yourself quite so seriously—no one else does!

Most of us make products and services that help people feel better. It's not a matter of life or death, it's about improving someone's day. And if you can't relax and have a little bit of fun, you'll be boring. How does that help anyone?

THREE RULES OF LIFE (AND EVERYTHING ELSE)

1. *Your Attitude Is Your Life* You can choose your attitude. And your attitude changes your life and the lives of those around you. Rarely does a bad attitude solve the problem. Typically, when something goes wrong or feels unpleasant, we get crabby and yell at the wrong people. We may solve the problem, but the crabbiness is an unnecessary extra. Solve the problem without the crummy attitude and everyone wins.

2. *Maximize Your Options* When we lock ourselves into one possibility of how things must be done, our businesses, our lives, and the lives of those around us get stuck. Maximize your options. Before you settle on just the right thing, play out a few more possibilities. In all things, big and small, open yourself to the possible options. Then trust yourself to choose the right one for the moment.

3. *Don't Let the Seeds Stop You From Enjoying the Watermelon* Tell this to yourself every day. It will help change your attitude. ;-)

CHEVY CHASE
AND BILL MURRAY

Chevy Chase has built his career around two words: "me" and "now." He was the first *Saturday Night Live* player to regularly use his name on television ("I'm Chevy Chase . . . and you're not.") and it made him the show's first star. He was the first to be featured solo in magazines and the first to leave the show for the movies.

Chevy's perspective was understandable. He didn't know how long he'd be a hot commodity, so he was in a hurry to cash in. Along the way, he developed a reputation as someone focused on *his* career and *his* sketches. The result was a career that started fast—and then stalled. Here are some of his more recent films: *Goose!*, *The Karate Dog*, *Bad Meat*, *Vacuums*, *Snow Day*, and *Dirty Work*.

Bill Murray was Chevy's replacement on the show. Bill got off to a very slow start. He hardly ever showed up on television. The writers didn't want to write for him, because they were comfortable with the stars they already had. Bill suffered for months.

Instead of throwing a tantrum, Bill chose to focus on the rest of the cast. He became friends (or lovers) with many of them, especially Gilda Radner. Over time, he built up a reputation as someone who could be counted on and trusted. When he was on camera, he wasn't the only one. He built his career with two words; they were "us" and "later."

Bill took the same approach to his movie career. The result? Murray's recent films couldn't be more different than Chevy's: *The Life Aquatic with Steve Zissou, Lost in Translation, The Royal Tenenbaums, Hamlet, Rushmore, Ed Wood,* and *Groundhog Day.*

Remarkable doesn't always mean right now.

THIS IS NOT ANOTHER "IPOD" STORY

Steve Jobs had a problem. His iPod was dominating the market, but was threatened by cheaper music players—players with far fewer features but much lower prices. He could stand his ground and lose market share, or go for the whole market and probably tarnish Apple's brand.

The iPod had a hard drive that was large but expensive. Would Apple compromise and turn the iPod into a commodity?

When Apple introduced the iPod Shuffle, it was clear that they had decided that giving less for less wouldn't do.

The original iPod had huge market share, but at $300 to $400, Apple's hard drive–based player was threatened by the Flash players that sold for a third that price. A Flash MP3 player uses a computer memory chip instead of a hard drive—so it's cheaper to make, but holds less music. Every day, more consumers were making a compromise and opting for the cheaper alternative.

Apple could have launched its own Flash player in response, but everything about it would have been a compromise in order to offer a lower price. A smaller, cheaper screen. A flimsier, cheaper body. A smaller, cheaper capacity.

So Apple did something different. They figured out how giving people less than what a Flash player offered could actually create a *better* product.

Apple removed the screen altogether. They made the player less than a third the size of the iPod and smaller than all of its competitors (the Shuffle weighs as much as a few sticks of gum). And most of all, they changed the way the user interacts with it. Instead of creating a player that houses and gives you complete access to all your music, the Shuffle grabs *some* of your music from your computer and then plays it back randomly. Like a radio station where you like all the songs.

Getting rid of the screen cut a huge piece out of Apple's costs, but it also allowed them to make a product that was not a compromise.

If you're an athlete or a commuter, this smaller, lighter, non-repetitive, no-skip player is actually *better* than the more expensive iPod. It's cheap and simple and you wear it around your neck. It doesn't skip and by forcing you to not make choices, it's more fun and easier to use.

You'll have to search far and wide to find a customer that doesn't want you to lower your prices. And most bosses are delighted to hear that you've figured out a way to cut costs.

But lower costs and lower prices usually mean products that are more average, less engaging, and involve big trade-offs for the user. Giving less for less is rarely a strategy for growth.

ING Direct uses the same strategy as Apple but in a very different business: banking. In three years, they've signed up more than a million new customers for their bank, largely based on what they *don't* do. They don't offer checking, they don't have ATMs, and they don't handle cash. They have no minimums and no fees. They don't have branches or tellers, either. In a few cities, you can visit an ING café for a latte and a mortgage, but that's it.

Instead, ING Direct puts the money they save into two things:

1. actual human beings who will talk to you instead of requiring you to go through a computer
2. higher interest rates

ING doesn't compromise in order to pay higher rates. They don't choose to give slightly less service, or to have people wait a little longer on hold. They don't put their branches in cheaper strip malls or use less carpeting in the lobby. They don't say, "Hey, what do you expect? We give better rates so you get less service!" Instead, they invented a bank where giving people less is actually *better*.

ING won't try to sell you a credit card, because they don't offer one. And they won't call you at home during dinner, because they don't do telemarketing.

As a result of their less-is-more, remarkable, big-moo strategy, an astonishing 40 percent of their new business comes from referrals. That means less money is needed for advertising. When they do spend money on advertising, they're able to get a new customer for a third of what it costs a traditional bank. Because they give fewer of the things we don't want, pay more interest, and charge lower fees.

No, this isn't about the iPod at all. It's about capitalizing on what you're good at, not compromising to be like the other guy.

A Miata isn't a cheaper, lesser Porsche. Southwest isn't a cheaper, lesser United. And Bic doesn't sell a cheaper, lesser Montblanc.

JUGGLING IS NOT WHAT YOU THINK IT IS

Sometimes, I teach juggling classes. Everyone wants to get the learning process of how to juggle three balls over with as quickly as he can. The universal approach people take is to devote all their attention and effort at catching the balls. They just throw 'em up and rush around trying to catch them. Extraordinary efforts are justified to catch the balls, because after all, if a ball hits the ground, you've failed. The nascent juggler expects that with enough practice, they'll get really good at catching balls.

Lots of your peers think that they're good at juggling. They rush this way and that, dealing with emergencies, handling multiple priorities, and never letting anything fall through the cracks.

But that's not juggling. That's rushing around like a madman. Let *them* be good at that. There are plenty of people out there who are great at rushing about and handling emergencies, and frankly, they don't need your help.

It turns out that juggling is about throwing, not catching. The way to learn how to juggle is not to focus obsessively on not dropping a ball. No, the way to get good at juggling is to focus on your throws instead.

If you are good at throwing, the catching will take care of itself.

Once you've got three or four or five projects in the air at work, no amount of rushing around is going to keep them from crashing to the ground. No amount of effort can help you catch the misthrown balls. It's physically impossible.

On the other hand, if your balls are well thrown, the catching is effortless.

That's part of the secret of becoming remarkable. Don't spend any time at all worrying about catching. Let your co-workers do that. Instead, become the best thrower there ever was. If you become good at throwing, you'll find that you're irreplaceable. Organizations need really good throwers.

MAKING THE WRONG DECISIONS, SLOWLY

How did TiVo end up on death's doorstep?

Here's a company that reinvented the single biggest influence in our world—television. A company that figured out how to make television work for the viewer, instead of the other way around. TiVo created a magical brand, secured a powerful licensing alliance, and had a huge impact on our culture—all with just a few hundred employees.

And yet they're out of money, can't keep a CEO, and are in danger of disappearing altogether.

The problem is that TiVo got scared. After they made it over the first few hurdles of financing and product development, they became focused on not blowing it.

Here they were, on the edge of greatness. They had enough money, enough time, and enough resources to get everything right. So they took it slowly and carefully, focusing on not making a mistake.

And that was the mistake.

Fail fast and cheap. Fail often. Fail in a way that doesn't kill you.

This is the only way to learn what works and what doesn't. TiVo had one remarkable idea, but they needed far more than that. You are going to make wrong decisions, no question about it. Make them fast and cheap.

BOB WEARS PANTY HOSE

In the early nineties, the brand managers, advertising execs, and manufacturing engineers that made L'eggs panty hose were almost exclusively middle-aged men. These men decided just how high the control top should ride on a woman's waist and divined the demand for a reinforced toe. Many based their decisions upon past sales, retailer demands, and competitive offerings. Others, like Bob, occasionally wore the product to try to understand how design changes affected comfort. For all his good intentions, Bob's natural plumbing prevented him from truly understanding the wonderful benefits of an improved cotton panel.

Doug, who worked for L'eggs's ad agency, did something better. He continually sought a woman's perspective. Doug would insist on conducting and attending user focus groups. He'd poll his wife, female co-workers, and even his mother almost daily. He made it his job to listen to people who actually wore panty hose.

Doug was a good marketer. He asked the women lots of

questions. He listened very closely to their concerns, comments, and suggestions. He acted upon this knowledge.

As marketers, we love to talk to ourselves. We love to talk to our colleagues, our peers, and our bosses. But many times we forget to talk to our customers.

We forget who our customers are, how they use our products, and how they relate to our companies. It's evident in the way our communication with them is filled with industry jargon and boardroom buzzwords. We forget *how* to talk to them.

When we fail to make the effort to do a good job talking to our customers, do we show them that we care about them—or that we care about our business? Talking to your customers can be hard. It takes hard work to seek out your fans, ask them the right questions, and come up with the best solutions to meet their needs. Hard work indeed, but *not* talking to your customers is even harder, because when you lose touch with them, you lose their business.

Truly remarkable businesses never lose touch with their customers. Remarkable companies remember to make and sell what their customers want to buy. Remarkable companies create advertising that strikes an emotional chord in the hearts of their customers. Like Doug, they stay relevant by remembering to continually ask, listen, and act.

Do you know who you're talking to? Do you speak their language? Or are you just babbling to yourself?

It's easy to be remarkable when you can truly connect with your customers; it's hard when you can only relate to the person in the mirror.

CARE!

That, in just one word, seems to be the essence of good customer service.

There are tons of books about measurement and strategy and management techniques. There are people who will monitor your phone logs, or do post-sale questionnaires. Car dealers have people calling folks a week later to be sure the service was good.

You could spend all your money and all your time trying to improve your customer service through one fancy technique or another.

Or you could just care. And hire people who care.

Caring goes a long way. Caring shows up in your tone of voice, your interactions, and your policies. Caring is the difference between a simple, easy form and a three-page government interrogation. Caring is the difference between treating every stranger as a potential customer instead of as a potential thief.

Have you ever been to a restaurant where they care? Or a hospital? You can tell immediately.

When I went to the cemetery a few months ago for the unveiling of my grandmother's tombstone, it was closed. On the window of the office was an 11 × 17-inch Xerox copy, one-tenth the actual size, of a map showing the location of every plot. The copy was so small that it was almost impossible to read. And the organization of the numbers was virtually random, so there was no way to find what we were looking for anyway.

The cemetery people knew we were coming. There were only two ceremonies scheduled that day, yet there was no note.

My family spent an hour, in the rain, walking up and down and back and forth looking for the plot. No luck. All because no one cared.

A minute before we were about to give up, the caretaker came by and asked if we needed help. He recognized the name and took us right over to my grandmother's plot. He cared. It showed. He wasn't doing this because he'd get a bonus. He was doing it because it was the right thing to do.

DEFYING GRAVITY

No one understands gravity. We don't know what makes it work or why it exists. No matter . . . it's here and we better get used to it. Some of us even enjoy it. Mission: Space, a ride at Disney's Epcot Center gives the rider two Gs of force. Disney even promises nausea, at no extra charge.

While fighting gravity is a fact of life, escaping it is almost impossible. Organizations have their own G forces. First, the existing business accelerates forward. Then, as it gathers momentum, external and organizational forces press down upon anyone with a new idea and pin him in place.

What does it take to defy corporate gravity?

Just like a rocket ship, the only way to break free of the gravitational field holding you back is to have enough acceleration. Bringing remarkable ideas to market depends on the acceleration of the vehicle transporting them, you. Simply discovering a great idea is not enough to free it from the gravitational forces in the organizational atmosphere. Birds and rockets have to provide force to fight against gravity, and you do too. Here are some strategies you can use to gain acceleration.

Commitment Will Focus Your Force

There's only so much energy you can put into your job, and focusing all of it in one place will dramatically increase your power. Even more important, your commitment will protect the core of remarkableness at the center of your idea.

As an idea passes through the layers of management and stakeholders in an organization, there is a tendency to negotiate changes as you drive for approval. Just as the edges of a rocket heat up and deform in the atmosphere, your concept will be pushed and molded around the edges as it accelerates.

As long as the changes don't impact the creative essence of the idea, you're fine. Creatives at the ad agencies work in the idea business. If they can't get excited about your idea, get worried. Some time ago I arrived early to a kickoff meeting for a new product and had a cup of coffee with the head creative. As I explained the idea we were meeting about, he asked me, "Why is this a good idea?" He rolled his eyes at my response about product convenience and responded with an "oh" that landed with a thud. His challenge still pops into my head every time I look at a new idea.

Sometimes, though, the atmosphere wins. The remarkability of your idea is squeezed out of it long before it hits the market. That's when it's time to abandon ship. It's not worth your time or the company's money. Without the significant element of the idea, it will lack market momentum and consequently fail to deliver the return on investment you need.

Emotions Are the Only Reason to Change

Numbers-based innovations are easy to sell. Eliminate the outer carton of the bottle, bundle multipacks together for Costco, or bring on another flavor. Do this and we'll save money. Sure! But numbers-based innovations are rarely home runs. They rarely cause people to look back in awe at the amazing thing they've done. It's the emotional stuff—the stuff that some smart people don't think will work—that you need to be part of.

The higher up the food chain the decision makers sit, the further away they are from the experience of the user. You can streamline your journey by showing them what excited you about the idea. The best way is to show them in person. Put them in front of a real customer experiencing your innovation. If you can't do that, put the customer's experience on video. Seeing the reaction on a consumer's face is extraordinarily influential, particularly in this opt-in world we live in. Once people see what you see, the shorter the distance your idea has to travel. The less distance, the fewer compromises, and the greater the speed.

As You Gain Momentum, Don't Forget to Fight Friction

At the same time you are trying to accelerate your idea, deceleration is occurring elsewhere because of proliferation and oversupply. Consider the toothpaste market as an example. We grew up with Crest and Colgate. Today there are hundreds of flavor and formula combinations to choose from, in every color imaginable. For a competitor to echo your last great idea is easy. So the market gets crowded.

You can join the crowd, but then you'll fail. Instead, you have to fight internal gravity. Putting a new toothpaste in a clear box with a nonmint flavor, for example, requires new connections and new resources. Just stand in front of a committee of manufacturing managers with your idea and you will feel how tethered your organization is to the current capital equipment and processes. Linking a big idea to the overall business strategy is one way to assuage the fears that inevitably arise among custodians of the core capabilities of the company.

Acknowledge That Your Rocket Isn't Perfect

Smart people know that even great ideas have downsides or compromises, and they worry about risk. By sharing the negative aspects of an idea up front, it puts the quality of the idea in context. Let them see why the idea is polarizing. When you openly discuss these issues, it will quiet the cynics and help them to see that you are promoting a significant idea, not just selling them on your opinions. Ethnic marketing is a great example. If you develop products for Hispanics, you don't expect non-Hispanic customers to go for them. It's the same for remarkable ideas. You have to find a big enough group that believes in the idea and not worry about all the others who don't.

Delivering a remarkable idea into the marketplace is a thrill. It's like barreling down the slope on a roller coaster with your arms thrust above your head while you join the other riders in a primal scream. As the car slows and stops at the bottom, the only thing you have on your minds is getting back in line to ride again!

WHAT ARE YOU MEASURING?

According to *Car and Driver* magazine, there's no real comparison between a 2005 Corvette and a Porsche 911. The Corvette is faster from zero to sixty, faster in the quarter mile, and faster to stop. The Corvette is better on the skid pad. And it costs about 38 percent less than the Porsche.

Given all of the obvious advantages of the Corvette, why did more than thirty thousand ostensibly rational North Americans buy a Porsche last year instead? That's a lot of cars.

It's unreasonable to assume that 1,800,000,000 (1.8 billion) dollars' worth of cars were purchased just because some middle-aged dentists were in love with a storied brand. Something else is going on.

It turns out that a hard-to-measure attribute called "path accuracy" is important here. A Porsche goes where you put it. The car (whether it's the big Cayenne or the sloopy 911) gives its driver a magical feeling of control. Just because this feeling is hard to measure, though, doesn't mean it's not real. It's so real that car buyers spend more than a billion dollars a year for it.

In a metric-minded organization, it's very tempting to focus on things that are easy to measure instead of those things that are *important* to measure.

HELL'S ANGELS AT THE CAPTAIN'S TABLE

Steve Wallach is reinventing the billion-dollar cruise industry. So is Judy Dlugacz. And neither one of them owns a boat. They work with existing lines and shake things up.

Steve worked for two years to get the approvals necessary to run his Harley-Davidson cruise. Dozens of Harley owners pay a substantial premium for the right to bring their own motorcycles along on his Caribbean cruises. They're first off the boat, roaring in a two-wide formation through the rural roads of islands like St. Maarten. Along the way, the Harley cruisers stop by cockfighting emporiums and hang out at the local equivalent of biker bars.

Slightly more sedate, Judy's group—Olivia Cruises and Resorts—is one of the fastest-growing businesses in the San Francisco Bay Area. She books ten thousand lesbians a year on affinity cruises that are joined by celebrities like K. D. Lang and Melissa Etheridge.

While Olivia's didn't worry about having to get a permit for one-thousand-horsepower motorcycles, Judy still wrestled with the inertia and risk aversion of an established industry. In both cases, though, it was this inertia that made the new ventures successful. If the people who owned cruise ships were willing to take actions they perceive as risks, there'd be no room for middlemen like Steve Wallach and Judy Dlugacz.

According to Douglas Ward, a best-selling author on cruises, "People get tired of standing in lines and being highly structured." He's convinced that much of the growth in the industry is going to come from the interesting fringes, not from the boring center.

PLANT ROCKS

Archaeologists working at the mysterious Easter Island in the Pacific were puzzled by the fact that what appeared to be ancient farmland was strewn with rocks. The presence of rocks seemed to belie the explanation that these were high-yielding farms feeding thousands of people. After all, the people of Easter Island had had thousands of years to improve the quality of their farms—and plenty of reason to do so, as it appears that they starved to death. For a time, these farms probably fed the entire island's population quite productively. Jared Diamond talks about the solution to the puzzle of the rocks in his book *Collapse*.

Anyone who has ever spent a summer hauling rocks to clear a farm in New Hampshire would know that the best farmland is free of rocks, stumps, and stones, making it easy to plow and harvest. Why were the ancient farms at Easter Island corrupted by easily removable rocks?

Research by scientists around the world has shown that successful farms in Peru, China, New Zealand, and Israel are set up the same way. It turns out that planting rocks in a semiarid area can transform a desert or arid plain into a productive farm. The rocks warm the soil by absorbing sunlight all day and releasing its heat at night. They collect dew and create pockets of moisture underneath. The rocks also prevent dusty topsoil from eroding as quickly, and they even add a bit of fertilizer to the soil.

Research into farming techniques used by the Anasazi Indians discovered that planting rocks increased the yield on every single one of the sixteen crops they grew. In fact, the average increase was 400 percent. Rocks, far from being an impediment, were the only reason that some cultures were able to farm at all.

All day, organizations like yours are busy making themselves more efficient, removing every impediment and noncontributing element they can find. The goal, it seems, is to create a pasture that's pristine, easy to plow, and optimally organized. Maybe, just maybe, that's not such a good idea.

Where are the rocks you've been clearing? What would happen if you put some back?

IS BIGGER BETTER?

On the inside of the original Macintosh computer casing, out of sight of all but the most aggressive hackers, lie about thirty-five signatures. Twelve of those are from the original Mac team.

It took only twelve people to build the hardware and software for the original Macintosh. Today, there are thousands of Apple employees working on the computer. It took less than a dozen people to invent the phenomenon of Starbucks. Room to Read, a successful new nonprofit out of San Francisco, is largely the work of one person—John Wood.

It's tempting to believe that the mighty R&D department of a Fortune 500 company is unbeatable, yet more often than you might imagine, great new innovations come from somewhere else. The Dyson vacuum wasn't invented by the engineers at Hoover or Miele. Wite-Out was invented by the mother of Michael Nesmith (the smartest Monkee), and the entire snowboarding industry was developed by Jake Burton.

Big organizations have a problem. The problem lies in handshakes. A group of two people needs only one meeting to exchange information. Fifty people, on the other hand, need 1,225 one-on-one meetings to have a similar exchange. Things can't help but slow down.

If you want to do something really extraordinary, take a colleague and set up your office in the Kinko's across the street. Come back to headquarters when you're done.

PLAY

play is tactile . . .

play is active . . .

play is experiential . . .

play is imaginative . . .

play is collaborative . . .

play is necessary . . .

play is unpredictable . . .

play is inventive . . .

play is community . . .

play is creative . . .

play is nimble . . .

play is emotional . . .

play is loud . . .

play is spontaneous . . .

play is serious business . . .

play is physical . . .

play is fun . . .

play is revealing . . .

play is cultural . . .

play is knowledge . . .

play is curious . . .

play is skill building . . .

play is imagination . . .

play is social . . .

play is instinctual . . .

play is art . . .

play is messy . . .

play is innovation . . .

play is terrifying . . .

play is joyful . . .

play is discovery . . .

play is challenging . . .

play is relaxing . . .

play is purposeful . . .

play is serious in business . . .
play is the unknown . . .
play is making mistakes . . .
play is freedom . . .
play is resourceful . . .
play is wise . . .
play is chaos . . .
play is untapped . . .
play is laughter . . .
play is boundless . . .
play is "Aha!" . . .
play is multisensory . . .
play is primal . . .
play is timeless . . .

play is movement . . .
play is forgotten . . .
play is marvelous . . .
play is energizing . . .
play is soulful . . .
play is permissive . . .
play is strategic . . .
play is a living lab . . .
play is problem solving . . .
play is visual . . .
play is the mother of
   invention . . .
play is genius . . .

VERSION 1.0

You probably don't know who created the first online bookstore (hint: It wasn't Jeff Bezos). And it's pretty unlikely that you're still using one of the first Internet search engines or even the first Web browser. Four years ago, a free software program called Napster started a revolution. Not long after, the company it spawned closed its doors. In each case, a revolutionary new idea was unleashed, and in each case, the first iteration of the idea failed. It was only after someone came and tried again, refining the idea in future incarnations, that the true potential was realized. It wasn't that the first try wasn't groundbreaking, or that people weren't excited about the possibilities. *Version one just wasn't good enough.*

The second best thing you can say about an idea is, "That's been done before, and it worked."

The best thing you can say is, "That's been done before, and it didn't work. . . . Let's do it again, but better."

DAVID (AND GOLIATH)

"If Greyhound wasn't a giant, maybe they could beat us . . . But because they are a giant, they cannot," says Shui Ming Zheng.

Zheng runs the Eastern Bus Company, which will happily transport you from Boston to Washington, D.C., by bus for ten dollars. Greyhound is paying too many people and has too much overhead to even consider a similar project. JetBlue wins with the same game plan. So did Wendy's, when McDonald's couldn't coordinate well enough to launch a salad.

If the race goes to the swift, not the large, then this is good news for anyone who's not listed on the Fortune 500. The race is getting faster, and clueless big companies continue to miss the boat.

Access to assets is no longer the key to success. The will to implement is.

GREAT IDEAS IN BED

A celebrated therapist was on one of the many pop-psychology shows on TV a while back. He was talking about what it takes to be a great lover. The message from the therapist was very simple.

Here was a trained sex therapist (accidentally) describing a set of guidelines any organization could use for better customer service, sales, and marketing success. It was a far more useful approach than what you might find written in employee handbooks and in training programs.

What was the big secret the therapist had to share?

First you ask your partner what they like.

Then you give it to them.

Then you ask them if they liked it.

If they say yes, do it again. . . .

WHY ASK WHY?

The woman sitting next to me on an airplane had thin, sharpened spikes, two of them, eight inches long. They're called knitting needles, and they're allowed on the plane. The guy on the other side of the aisle was bemoaning the fact that they took away his nail clippers.

The little kid in row 8 had to walk thirty-five rows to the back of the plane to use the bathroom because it's a grave breach of security for him to use the empty bathroom just seven rows in front.

They x-ray sneakers at LaGuardia.

My hotel sent me down the street to a health club because the hotel's workout room was under construction. The health club wouldn't let me use the facilities until I filled out a form with my name and full address and contact information. Why? "Insurance regulations." Apparently, this is the same reason you can't watch the mechanic repair your car or visit the kitchen of the local restaurant.

My doctor's office doesn't have a fax machine.

The stellar Maison du Chocolat café in New York doesn't serve herbal tea.

The government of New York State makes it illegal to buy wine on the Internet.

Why? I have no clue. Neither do the people implementing these policies. Go ahead, ask them. They'll tell you how maddening it is to be asked over and over again and have no answer.

If your front-line people are unable to answer a "why" question, what do you tell them to do? Standard operating procedure is to bluff, stall, or ignore the question.

Most bureaucracies don't want the *whys* working their way up the chain. Most bureaucracies encourage people in the field to be the first and only line of defense. "That's our policy." "I'm sorry, but there's nothing I can do about that." "Insurance regulations, sir." The goal is to get the customer (questioner) to go away.

To go away.

They want you to go away.

Does that make any sense at all? The single most efficient (and inexpensive) technique for improving your operations is answering the "why" questions! You should embrace these people, not send them away.

"You know, sir, I have no idea why you have to do that. But I can tell you that I'll find out before the end of the day."

The moment you start treating your people like people (as opposed to cogs), they're likely to start acting like people. And when that happens, things will begin to improve.

The price of being a sheep is BOREDOM. The price of being a Wolf is LONELINESS. Choose one or the other with great CARE.

© gapingvoid.com

TALKING ABOUT THE WEATHER

Until I was thirty-five years old I thought talking about the weather was for losers. A waste of time, insulting even. No one can do anything about the weather anyway. I believed that any comment that doesn't offer new insight or otherwise advance the cause of humanity is just so much hot air. I might make an exception among intimate friends, but I sure did not want that kind of intimacy with the man on the street, or the one in my office.

Then something happened. Alone for the first time in a long time, living in challenging circumstances (a truck), experiencing a cold winter in New England, I noticed the weather. It affected me deeply and directly, every single day. Slowly it dawned on me that the weather affected everyone else, too. Maybe talking about it wasn't totally vacuous after all.

I started with the cashier at a gas station. I figured I'd never see her again, so it was pretty safe. She had no clue that I lived in my truck or that I was a smart person with a lot of potential. Years of cynicism made me almost laugh as I said, "Sure got a lot of snow this year so far." "Yep," was her reply. Then she said, "I could barely get my car out of the lot, be careful driving!" Talking about the weather was easy, even effortless. An entrée to at least one person on the planet who apparently cared about me, at least enough to share her small challenge and want me safe on the road. Wow.

Next I tried it out at work. It turned out to be even more effective with people I already knew. Talking about the weather acted as a little bridge, sometimes to further conversation and sometimes just to the mutual acknowledgement of shared experience.

Whether it was rainy or snowy or sunny or damp for everyone, each had their own relationship with the weather. They might be achy, delighted, burdened, grumpy, relieved, or simply cold or hot. Like anything of personal importance, most were grateful for the opportunity to talk about it.

Then something else happened. As talking about the weather became more natural, I found myself talking about a whole lot more. Cashiers and clients and suppliers and colleagues all over opened up about all kinds of things. I found out about peoples' families, their frustrations at work, their plans and aspirations. Plus, I found out that the weather is *not* the same for everyone! And it's only one of many factors dependent on location that you'll never know about without engaging in casual conversation.

For a businessperson, there may be no better way to make a connection, continue a thread, or open a deeper dialogue. Honoring the simple reality of another person's experience is an instant link to the bigger world outside one's self. It's the seed of empathy, and it's free.

Why Talking About the Weather is Good
- Weather is egalitarian in its delivery.
- Weather is fundamentally inoffensive.
- Weather is completely accessible.
- No one is ignorant about weather.
- Even shy people are willing to share their personal feelings about the weather.
- It's hard not to smile when you ask "Hot enough for you?"

How Talking About the Weather Can Change Your Life
Organizations are about a lot more than just completing tasks. We spend a lot of time with our co-workers, and many of our trusted relationships are here. If you can't talk about the weather with your co-workers, what chance do you have of getting them to believe in you? Talking about the weather is a baby step on your way to making change.

Now I can barely remember what it was like to get through the day without talking about the weather. Wherever you are in your career, in any role or setting, try it out. Walk right up to just about anyone and say, "I sure am happy to see the sun."

NO GUARANTEES

For eighteen years, David Atkinson pursued a remarkable project.

He wanted to know what the winds were like on Titan, the largest moon of Saturn. Working at the University of Idaho, Atkinson pursued his quixotic quest for nearly two decades, never even certain that we'd send a ship there, or if his experiment would be included.

You can bet David got a hard time from his peers and his family. "Why can't you work on something more normal?" they probably wanted to know. But he persisted, confident in his quest to unlock Titan's mysteries.

Finally, the European Space Agency announced plans to send a probe to Titan. David submitted his work and they accepted his experiment. A joint venture with NASA and the Italian space agency, the probe was designed to discover the secrets of the ringed planet and its moons.

Atkinson's experiment would use two channels of radio data

to report back the results of the Doppler wind tests. Channel A was the important one, with B acting as a secondary, lesser source of data.

Someone forgot to turn on Channel A.

"I (and the rest of my team) waited and waited and waited," Atkinson wrote. "We watched the probe enter and start transmitting data, but our instrument never turned on . . . We do have Channel B data and although driven by a very poor and unstable oscillator, we may be able to get a little bit of data.

"I think right now the key lesson is this—if you're looking for a job with instant and guaranteed success, this isn't it."

That's something worth thinking about, isn't it? If you're looking for a job with instant and guaranteed success, where exactly *are* you going to look? Does a job like that exist? If it did, would it be worth having?

Too often, we forget about the journey and worry instead about the guarantees and the risks and the home run. David Atkinson, in his moment of greatest frustration, discovered something different. He realized that the very lack of guarantees is what made the work so compelling. Eighteen years down the drain? Not really.

PERIODIC TABLE OF DIFFERENTS

FUNCTION	BIG COMPANY	START-UP
Positioning	Being all things to all people	Finding a niche and dominating it
Pitching	Sixty slides, 120 minutes, and fourteen-point font	Ten slides, 20 minutes, and thirty-point font
Business planning	Two hundred pages of extrapolation from historical data	Twenty pages of wishful thinking
Bootstrapping	Staying in a Hyatt Regency instead of a Ritz Carlton	Staying with a college buddy instead of a Motel 6
Recruiting	Corporate headhunters screening candidates with Fortune 500 or Big Four track records	Sucking in people who "get it" and are willing to risk their careers for stock options
Partnering	Negotiating I-win, you-lose deals that the press will like	Finding a way to increase sales by piggybacking on others
Branding	Advertising during the Super Bowl	Evangelizing in the trenches
Rainmaking	Spiffs for resellers and commissions for sales reps	Sucking up, down, and across
Existing	Calling the legal department for advice	Helping people who can't (apparently) help you
Researching	Buying books by the boxful	Borrowing a buddy's and photocopying it for everyone

READY OR NOT! IN DEFENSE OF YOUR OWN READINESS

Are you ready? Ready to take the plunge? To do an original, life-affirming, remarkable thing? Are you ready to risk living a remarkable life? The German philosopher-poet Goethe gave us the only bit of wisdom you need:

"Whatever you can do, or dream, *begin it*. Boldness has genius, magic, and power in it. Begin it now."

"But wait," you say to Goethe, even though he says "begin it" twice to you, "I'm not ready."

Well, you're wrong. Terribly wrong.

1. You Don't Need . . .

- A life of quiet desperation. Not now, not ever.
- Permission—it's highly overrated. Imagine Steve Jobs seeking permission.
- A lot of fancy moves—Duke Ellington only had four.
- More experience. Beginning it is the experience.
- To forgive yourself for the things you've screwed up. It's history.

- To be computer literate. The best decisions and the best ideas come from people, not machines.
- A degree. M.B.A.s and other three-letter words are also over-rated. Ask Tom Peters, who has three, and still got *fired* by McKinsey only to go on to become the big "!"
- Praise for your idea. Constructive criticism is a much more helpful filter.
- An invitation. Waiting to be asked to the table, the dance, the game, the party, the big meeting is a waste of important energy that keeps you from beginning.
- A baseline or benchmark. By the time you've baselined and benchmarked, it's already too late.
- Consensus—even if you buy the notion that consensus means 50 percent approval.
- Money. Bootstrapping is simply a design constraint.
- Gratitude. As I learned from both my father (who said this often when people whined in his business), and from my dear dog Topper, "If you want gratitude, get a dog."

2. You Do Need . . .
- Passion, to get you over the hurdles.
- Trust. Tiny threads of passion always lead to bigger threads.
- Attention. Watch out for the threads and they become tapestries.
- Guts to ask the question, "What's missing?"
- An attitude that suggests, "I'm prototyping, playing, and palling around."

- To arm yourself against perfectionists when you choose to use this attitude. They don't like it.
- The realization that learning is a paradox. It is life affirming and often painful, because you care, and without it you're literally dead.

3. How I Know You're Ready (to Be Remarkable)

Evidence for Adults
- You've dealt with life's big, complex challenges—in spite of many of your employers' attempts to infantilize you in the guise of "leadership."
- You've probably fallen in love at least once. At least at the movies.
- You've mastered the other big three: food, clothing, and shelter. I can tell, because you had enough disposable income to buy (or beg, borrow, or steal) this book.

Evidence for Kids
- You're a *kid*!
- Kids, by definition, *are* remarkable.

For Everyone Else Who Isn't Ready
- You've already begun.
- Readiness is overrated. Remember Goethe?

WHAT NOW?

Go do something remarkable. Buy books for everyone you work with. Go do something else remarkable. Repeat.

ABOUT THE AUTHORS:
THE GROUP OF 33

Alan Webber was cofounder of *Fast Company* magazine, which changed everything. He is currently working on Blue Letter, a new project that uses social intelligence to change the world's business conversation.

Amit Gupta was cofounder of The Daily Jolt and managing editor of www.changethis.com. When he was ten, he built a working time machine. He is currently working on his next start-up. Visit him at www.amitgupta.com.

April T. Armstrong is a professional actress, singer, and storyteller. She also writes and directs for the theater. She is a teaching artist and curriculum consultant for various arts-in-education programs.

Carol Cone has been called the mother of cause marketing. Her first experience with social issues was at Brandeis during the 1970 national student strike. She sat in, but didn't burn, any buildings. She is the founder of Cone, Inc., in Boston. (www.coneinc.com)

Chris Meyer is the coauthor of the bestseller *Blur* and the pathbreaking *It's Alive*, which presents our best understanding of how biological principles apply to management. He has recently become chief executive of Monitor Networks, a venture designed to improve the mobility of human capital. (www.themonitornetworks.com)

Daniel H. Pink is the best-selling author of *Free Agent Nation* and *A Whole New Mind*. Earlier in his career he wrote speeches for Al Gore and dug pit latrines in Botswana, though not at the same time. (www.danpink.com)

Dave Balter is the founder of Bzz-Agent and openly admits his addiction to all things word-of-mouth. He is coauthor of the upcoming book *Grapevine*. (www.bzzagent.com)

Dean DeBiase has run Fortune 500 subsidiaries and several innovative companies, including Autoweb, which he took public and merged with Autobytel, and Imagination Network, which he sold to AOL. He's the cofounder of Startup Partners and Remarkabalize.com and developing a new book—*Reboot Your Organization!*

Donna Sturgess is vice president of innovation at GlaxoSmithKline. She knows a lot about marketing consumer brands, like toothpaste, and what it takes to bring something great to market. Donna transmits creative energy! sturgessdonna@yahoo.com

Guy Kawasaki evangelized the Macintosh to success and is a best-selling author of several books, including *The Art of the Start*. He's also a successful speaker and venture capitalist. (www.garage.com)

Heath Row is editorial and community director for *Fast Company*. He hopes to meet you some day. (www.fastcompany.com)

Jackie Huba is coauthor of the best seller *Creating Customer Evangelists*. She is a respected speaker and consultant. (www.churchofthecustomer.com)

Jacqueline Novogratz is the founder of the Acumen Fund. She is in the vanguard of changing the way we look at helping the developing world become part of the global marketplace. (www.acumenfund.org)

Jay Gouliard is vice president of packaging development at General Mills and former wizard of WOW! at Coca-Cola. He leads the team that launched a new package format for kids' yogurt creating a hundred-million-dollar brand called Go-GURT that dominates

the category today. (www.genmills
.com)

Julie Anixter was managing director of the Tom Peters Company
and is now director of brand experience at LAGA, where she con-
sults, writes, and speaks about
brands, inside and out. She is also
the cofounder of remarkabalize.com.
(www.laga.com)

Kevin Carroll was an evangelist at
Nike and now runs his own consulting firm, The Katalyst Consul-
tancy. Kevin teaches people how to
play again. He is the author of
*Rules of the Red Rubber Ball: Find
and Sustain Your Life's Work.*
(www.katalystconsultancy.com)

Lisa Gansky was cofounder of
GNN, the first commercial Web
site, vice president of Internet stuff
at AOL, then cofounder of Ofoto.
Now, freshly departed from Ko-
dak/Ofoto, she's focusing on
www.dosmargaritas.org, Get Active
Software, and Simo Health. Lisa's
a self-declared "impact junkie."

Lynn Gordon is the creator of
the wildly successful 52®activity
decks. She is also an inventor,

author, and nonprofit founder.
(www.girlsource.org)

Malcolm Gladwell is a writer for
The New Yorker and the author of
The Tipping Point and *Blink.* His
books have sold far more than a
million copies.
(www.gladwell.com)

Marc Benioff is the founder of
www.salesforce.com. He is well-
respected for integrating social responsibility into his company.

Marcia Hart is a half-funky
and half-corporate architect who
matches business plans with space
requirements. She and her partner
live like shoemaker's children in a
big old brownstone in Baltimore
that is under constant renovation—
by their own hammers!
(www.azimuthgroup.com)

Mark Cuban is owner of the NBA
Mavericks, founder of Broadcast
.com (which he sold to Yahoo for
billions of dollars) and HDnet, and
a successful speaker and TV per-
sonality.

Polly LaBarre is a business journal-
ist, explorer, and pattern recognizer.

She has three questions: What makes the most vital organizations tick? How do the highest-impact people work? And who has the most fun in the process? She was senior editor of *Fast Company* magazine in its early days and is currently working on a book called *Mavericks at Work* (forthcoming from William Morrow).

Promise Phelon is leading the movement to eradicate customer abuse. Her firm, The Phelon Group helps large technology companies leverage their customer relationships as assets rather than commodities. (www.phelongroup.com)

Randall Rothenberg is the director of intellectual capital at Booz Allen Hamilton. The firm's former chief marketing officer, he is a columnist for *Advertising Age* magazine, a former media and marketing reporter for *The New York Times,* and the author of *Where the Suckers Moon: The Life and Death of an Advertising Campaign.*

Red Maxwell is president of on-ramp Branding and made the world safe for preppies by starting the advertising design and photog-

raphy departments at Polo Ralph Lauren. He does his most important work with the Juvenile Diabetes Research Foundation. (www.onrampbranding.com)

Robin Williams is one of the best-selling computer book authors ever. *The Little Mac Book* is widely regarded as the classic of the genre. Her latest book is about Shakespeare's true identity.

Robyn Waters is the person who turned Target Stores into a style mecca. She now runs her own consulting firm. Her new book, *The Trendmaster's Guide: Get a Jump on What Your Customer Wants Next* comes out this year. (www.rwtrend.com)

Seth Godin is the author of seven books that have been best sellers around the world, including three *New York Times* best sellers. He insists that he is naturally bald. (www.sethgodin.com)

Tim Manners is the editor of Cool News of the Day, the most influential marketing newsletter online. You really should get a free subscription. (www.reveries.com)

Tom Kelley is general manager at IDEO, a red-hot center for design and innovation. He swore *The Art of Innovation* would be "absolutely, positively" the only book he'd ever write. His next one comes out later this year. (www.ideo.com)

Tom Peters is the best-selling business book author of all time. He has reinvented and reimagined the way we work. Tom is the reason the rest of us get to write. (www.tompeters.com)

William Godin is the president of HARD Manufacturing, the world's largest fabricator of hospital cribs. He is not the founder of this 129-year-old company. He has received numerous honors for his work with community organizations in Buffalo, New York. (www.hardmfg.com)

ABOUT THE ILLUSTRATOR

Hugh MacLeod draws cartoons on the backs of business cards. He also helps run a bespoke Savile Row tailoring firm. Sometimes he's a "blogvertising" consultant as well, helping clients use blogs to spread commercial ideas (as opposed to commercial messages, which is a different thing altogether). www.gapingvoid.com.

ACKNOWLEDGMENTS

This book is dedicated to you. *But only if you help.*

How can you help? You can help the cause and you can help the world if you'll just buy ten copies of this book and give them to your boss, your employees, your co-workers, or anyone else who could use a little remarkable in their lives.

The good news is that it's a selfish gesture as well. Your life will get way more interesting if you can help your friends stop trying to be perfect.

This book is also dedicated to the people who wrote it. Every single one did it for free. Without hesitation. Thanks, guys.

Particular thanks to the folks at Portfolio, especially Megan Casey, who gets it.